MW01443390

Sweet Strength

SEASIDE AWAKENINGS

LINDA TIMMONS

Independently Published
Sweet Strength | Mount Pleasant, SC

ISBN: 9798622777165

Dedication

To my loving husband, Mark (November 13, 1958 - January 9, 2012). My knight in shining armor. Everyone's best friend, the wind beneath my wings. My Sweet Strength. You encouraged me to write. This is for you. I love you. To my son, Robert, my joy and my hero. I love you more than you will ever know.

Table of Contents

Foreword

"I must be a mermaid…I have no fear of depths and a great fear of shallow living." The Four- Chambered Heart, in Cities of the Interior, pg.249 Anais nin

"After a while I discard a dress not because it is worn (I cannot wear out my dresses, I hardly fray them) but because of the self which enjoyed that particular dress has changed, has outworn it, needs to assume another color, another shape." Diary 5, pg 194

Anais Nin

Many thoughts and emotions have run through my mind as I wrote this foreword. I wanted to write this to let you know that there is hope and a new life, if you so desire, after grief, after loss, after pain and after change of unpredictable circumstances.

As I look, read and reflect back upon those painful moments of time and season I suddenly realize the passage of growth and strength that grief took me through. It has been eight years now or eight seconds depending on how you allow your mind to grasp it. In those years was the time it took to find my new normal and grow beyond guilt, pain, regret and struggle. It was also finding who I was in the midst of the unknowing.

Our beliefs about death and living will either destroy us or propel us to a higher place. I believe that God always wants to propel us to a higher place, a happier place and a peaceful place if we allow Him. However, I also believe it is always in our hands, our eternal vision and in the reaction that we have after the worst circumstances we thought possible. We will either bend, break or become.

I hope after reading this you will become a better person and not bitter. I hope you become a victor not a victim and that you can take all of your pain and recycle it to help others with their pain. I do believe this is how God will ultimately heal you and has healed me. I hope that, in spite of the darkness, you will find God is the one who holds the light for you because he is light and love. I hope that you will ask questions and not think that you have all the answers spun on that weave of faithless doubt. The faithless doubt that if God loved you this would not have happened. I hope that it brings you to the point of searching for love, not running from it.

Life worth living is truly for those who experience death of loved ones, of possessions, failures and unexpected challenging circumstances.

I am now convinced that unless you face loss you cannot learn to live. I struggled more than people saw. I cried more than people knew. I was depressed, lost and lonely but hid it through a smile. There were times I was so much weaker than I was strong and certainly times I did not feel like being Sweet Strength nor was I. But through it all, I never gave up. I knew that God would provide even in my faithless battles with Him. I wrote my visions on index cards and carried them around with me. I went to sunrises every morning on the beach so that I could hear God's mercy crying my mercies are new every morning. It is a new dawn and a new day. Get up and shine!

We can never understand what someone else goes through but you can be comforted in knowing that God does. My faith is my faith and yours may look different than mine and that is okay. You need to find your way. My walk was and still is through His son Jesus and His Amazing Grace. You have to find the hope and the light that will guide your way. I walked away from Him and from my faith many days. He never walked away from me. Everyone handles their grief differently and I wish I had a magic word that would empower you and strengthen you through your dark days but I do not. However, if you listen closely and become aware of your surroundings God will heal you where you are and where you go. He may speak to you through someone you least expect. He may speak to you through a book, a poem, a song or even nature. God can use any and all things to pull you back up. All you have to do is open the door to your heart and allow the healing in.

The good Lord has brought me through and to a new decade, a new life and a new identity. Here I am still standing strong and tall in 2020. So many good things have transpired in my years since writing this book. The experiences that unfolded have led to a new marriage, two step sons and owning my brick and mortar business Sweet Strength Fitness Studio.

On September 7th, 2017 I remarried, Breeze Timmons, (Herbert Anglo Timmons, III). We met again through his brother, Charles Timmons in April of 2017. Charles and I re-connected through facebook and I naturally asked about Breeze. Who knew I would be married four months later after Breeze's brother passed my number along. From the beginning we knew our relationship felt right. Breeze and I grew up together in a small town and school in Lake City, South Carolina. We lived in a town where everyone knew one another. Our school was very much the same. Breeze was one grade below me so we knew each other well. Both our parents played golf and cards together with other parents in the community. There is something to be said about knowing someone for so long. The connection and bond that you cannot explain and do not have with anyone else. The rest is history. Our whole story is for another book and another time. I wanted to let you know that love can happen again after the death of a spouse and it can be good. It will not be the same and nor should it be. It will be different and it will be good. You do have enough heart left to love again just as deeply as you did before.

As I previously mentioned, I inherited two step sons from Breeze. God provided me with a new family. I love these boys and they have brought such joy to my life. His youngest son, Hudson, is twelve years old and his oldest son, Joshua, is fifteen years old. I now have three sons. My son, Robert, is still serving in the military and I am so proud of him. He has always been there for me. He has carried me through when I used to carry him. He is my hero.

Lastly, I would like to make mention of the business, I bought in December 2019, Sweet Strength Fitness Studio. My "Cowboy" aka Breeze works here with me in Mount Pleasant, South Carolina. We both work together at the studio training and empowering people to a higher level.

There is a lot more to the story here but as I stated before it is for another book for a future time. I just wanted to let you know that if you are reading this you have a purpose in life to be lived. There is hope of another day and a new you. I look forward to writing my next book and inspiring others to get up and walk into their new visions and new dreams leaving the old dreams in the past where they belong.

Never ever give up on yourself or your dreams! Write a new story. The old story does not read well anymore and the pages are too worn to read. You cannot move forward if you are clinging to a past story.

Strong Soldiers

"Keep your head up, God gives his battles to the strongest soldiers."
—*Linda Timmons*

You are a strong soldier. Think about what you have been through and what you are going through. You were selected by the one who knows you better than you know yourself. You were selected by your Creator. Why? You were selected because you are a strong warrior. If you were not strong you would not have been chosen for such an important battle. The battle called LIFE. We are in a battle, a battle for our mindsets, a battle for our health and wellness, a battle for love, peace and God. He created the universe and knitted you together in the womb. God Himself, the King of Kings picked you! His strongest, most determined and most qualified soldier to fight the battle you are in. You are thinking, I did not ask for this battle. WOW! What an honor and privilege to know that while you may not have asked for it, you were qualified and specially picked—handpicked in fact—because God knew that you would not give up. He knew you could change the way the evil battle was going. He knew you could fight the battle because you had what it took in your heart and soul. You had passion because you believed there was a purpose and plan to this battle, this war. He also knew you had this battle in the palm of your hand because He has you engraved in the palm of His hand. You have already won! The best reward to winning the battle lies within your spirit, which lives on and loves on. You are a brave warrior and a strong soldier. Go for it and receive the reward that is waiting for you at the victory celebration, your real home.

Introduction

"I am certain that I never did grow in grace one – half so much anywhere as I have upon the bed of pain." —*Charles Spurgeon*

My first book is not like most because it outlines my journey over the last four years. A journey full of grief yet at the same time inspiring others through my passion and love of coaching. It is not a book to be read from beginning to end. It entails my daily thoughts as I traveled through so many losses and changes all while building my coaching business. My hope is that you will be inspired and encouraged by my journey. Through grief a new career was built in hopes to effectively benefit affect others along the way. May these writings on grief give you comfort as you walk through losses you may have experienced.

I do not call myself a Christian but a follower of Christ. He has been with me every step of the way and is the only person I have found who truly loved me unconditionally. This book is not intended to persuade you to turn your life over to Christ. You will have to find your own way to peace. My peace is Jesus Christ. This is simply my walk.

My healing and comfort came from the beach, watching the sunrise, surfing, walking, running, strength training and capturing sunsets. I wish I could have added all the sunrises I watched over the last four years but descriptions and images of them would fill this book and so many more. My healing also came through the support and encouragement of family, friends, and coaching others. This is why I believe so much in what I do and am so passionate about my work as a transformational coach. We are not alone in our journey. We are here to support and encourage one another. Everyone wants to be listened to, loved and valued for who we are; not who others think we should be or even who we think we should be but simply who we are today. In my experience there are no exceptions to this rule.

I have such a passion to empower others to take control of their lives from the inside out. We cannot control a lot of our circumstances but we can control how we react to and perceive them in our lives. Through the power that lies within us we can create who we want to be and how we want to live our lives.

As Napoleon Hill states in his book Think and Grow Rich, "You may see at one and the same time both your best friend and your greatest enemy, by stepping in front of a mirror." There is no truer statement. You are the only one in life with whom you will compete against. It is all in your thoughts, your belief systems and your paradigms that will reflect the one you see in the mirror. Your self-image and what you believe about the world around you as well as the experiences you go through, both good and bad, will determine how well you live your life. Only you can give yourself happiness, health and wealth. This is what I hope you gain after reading this book.

Thank you! I am sending blessings of peace, love, happiness, health, joy and wealth to every hand that holds this book. That is my desire for you that burns within me.

Mark the Shark

If I had one word to describe my husband Mark it would be the word loyal. He was loyal with his walk with Christ, he was loyal to his family, his friends and his love of surfing. I loved this about him.

There are so many things I loved about Mark. His blue eyes that held the depth of the ocean. His smile and laugh that would light up a room. The way he held me and kissed me. How he showed his love to me through his commitment and loyalty. His patience to stop and smell the roses. The way he could fully be with those who sat in front of him. His humor. The way he would say…whew doggie mama when I walked out of the room in the outfit he loved on me. The way he would go all out for anniversaries, Christmas, Valentines and birthdays. The way he would slow me down. His love for animals, he loved our dogs and would go to lengths to keep them healthy. His love of the ocean and nature. There are so many stories and memories that we shared together and a part that could fill many pages in a book. He was one of those people that make an indelible mark on your heart that can never be erased. Everyone loved Mark. You would be hard-pressed to find someone who didn't. In fact, I do not believe you could. As, the pastor said at the funeral, "I bet you all felt like you were Mark's best friend."

Mark was my rescuer. He was like the knight in shining armor that rode up on a white horse. Some of his friends said, "I rescued him." I beg to differ. I met Mark shortly thereafter and we married a year and a half later. In fact, when I was talking to my mom about this man I had met she said to me, "Does he have blonde hair and blue eyes?" I was taken back because I had not described him at all. I said, "Yes he does." She said, "When I was leaving your house the other day, I saw an image of a man with blonde hair and blue eyes. God, said to me, Linda is going to be alright." And...I was. You see this is the image that will always be in my heart. The knight in shining armor. When someone dies that you love, you never remember the bad. The good gets magnified, because you never truly know what you have until it's gone. We take so many things for granted and I took so many things for granted that I wish I could get back. You just never realize the sacredness of a marriage. When we did things together you understand that it wasn't just things or experiences it was so much more. When you lose someone you realize that the marriage you held was more than just two people saying vows together, it was a spiritual joining of two hearts joined in one God. It will drive you to your knees. The gratefulness of having experienced a marriage and having lived a life with another life so intimately. In the good times and the bad...we are still joined by one heart and one spirit. Yes, there are so many things I took for granted.

Like any married couple we had our good times and our bad times. We had times of adjustment but we always adjusted. We never gave up on each other. We were so different in so many ways. He was laid back and easy going and I was full of energy and movement. But, this is what made at the end of the day a great friendship and marriage. He would calm me down and I would, as he said, "Make him feel alive." I think I kept him on his toes and he kept me grounded on mine. I am so thankful for the influence Mark had on my life. The time I spent with him. I love him.

Mark had an instant family. I had one son, Robert. Robert was two and half when we met, and Mark loved him as his own. Robert thought of Mark like a dad. He called him Dad. They did what most dad and son's do but their special time was in the water surfing. That was Mark's love, surfing. He bought Robert his first board at nine years of age. Robert fell in love with surfing and to this day he has two of Mark's boards in which he treasures and surfs on.

Mark's love of surfing started when he was young. He went on to join the NSSA National Scholastic Surfing Team and won the NSSA National Championship in 1978. He was called "Mark the Shark" in the water and after he died my son had a shark tattooed on his back. When Mark died, we had a paddle out in his honor, the day after we had his celebration of life at the church. Surfers around the world practice this ritual, known as a memorial paddle out, usually to honor the life of a fallen surfer. There were probably a hundred surfers in the water and a hundred people on the beach to honor Mark. It was beautiful and it was the glue that kept me pieced together during that day. I had everyone sign his National Championship board at the celebration of life service and at the paddle out. The board use to hang on my wall over my bed as a comforting memoir of how special and loving my husband was. I treasured the significance and the love that was written in the signatures on that board.

Mark the Shark—November 13, 1958 to January 9, 2012—the legacy between the dash—will never be forgotten.

Part One:

Bereavement

"Blessed are those who mourn for they will be comforted."
—*Jesus*

What Now?

Mark, I miss you so much. I feel like my insides have been ripped out of me. Mark, my better half, you are gone and I cannot wrap my mind around it. I cannot sleep. Everyone has said such wonderful things about you because, well, you are wonderful. What am I going to do now? Mark…I love you. You were my best friend.

Rearrange

"Shock is a merciful condition. It allows you to get through disaster with necessary distance between you and your feelings."
—*Lisa Kleypus*

The Monday Mark passed away will forever be etched in my mind. It was an ordinary day, nothing spectacular. Mark had gone to a business meeting earlier and was home getting ready to take his daily run. I was studying and working on my business.

The previous night, while playing ping-pong, I noticed that Mark was sweating. It was a frigid January night, and we were outside playing. I asked him if he was all right and he said yes. I remember we had a fun night—probably the best time we had in a while. The whole day was great including playing ping pong. There was something very special about that day. It was as if God gave us a special day. We had gone to church earlier in separate cars. We were meeting friends for breakfast and I got there first. He pulled up, picked a plastic poinsettia flower that was lying on the sidewalk and handed it to me through the window. He said, "Here are your flowers today. Picked it just for you." I smiled and laughed. Little did

I know how much that flower, which could never die, would mean to me. Mark used to bring me fresh flowers a lot. He knew I loved flowers. He would surprise me with them and knew I loved to put them in our big bay windows in the living room. This was one of those little things that God gives you to show He loves you. We had a meal with two dear friends and then went home to our beachfront condo.

Monday came around as it comes every week. However, Monday, January 9th, 2012 was not just another Monday. Life brings with it unexpected experiences that forever change us, after which one could say, "That was the Monday my life was like this and this Monday my life is something different."

I went against my intuition, my spirit and my gut. Right before my husband left for his run he came in the office where I was diligently studying. Mark said, "I'm going for my run now." My gut told me to get up and hug him goodbye. Now, I do not usually hug him when he goes for a run. Because after all, I would see him after his run right? I sat there in my chair—the distance seems so foreign now—and said, "Have a good run baby." Oh, why did I not get up and hug him? It has taught me a lesson to listen to my gut, to listen to that voice inside.

About forty minutes later I heard the door open then this loud bump and a grunt, followed by a thud. I yelled out, "Mark, are you okay?" I went into the kitchen to discover Mark in convulsions with blue curled up fingers. It is a sight anyone would love to forget. He was swelling in his face and body. I thought he was having a seizure of some kind. I called 911 and they asked if I knew CPR. Yes, I did but I could not even think what to do. I was just in shock. My mind could not process what was happening. My heart hurt. I put the phone down and on speaker as I tried chest compression and breathing for him while waiting for the ambulance. It seemed time stopped and the seconds were hours but the paramedics arrived in a few minutes. I was yelling at Mark, screaming at him not to die. DO NOT DIE ON ME! I was breathing into hollowness. I was saying breathe Mark, come on breathe. The 911 operator kept asking me to feel for a pulse. My mind would trick me. I would feel a pulse and see him breathing but the reality was there was no pulse nor was he breathing. It was a complete nightmare. I could not grasp it. I mean forty minutes ago he was standing in front of me in his navy blue jogging pants and matching jacket talking to me. His voice. Talk to me Mark. Please, let me hear your voice. I never got to hear his voice again. Please God do not do this. Please do not let him die. In times like this you beg, plead and hope that God will work a miracle. The ambulance got to the house and worked on him for what seemed like hours. They finally put him on a stretcher and told me to follow them to the hospital. I asked if he would be all right and they said, "Ma'am, he is not breathing on his own but we will do the best we can."

I called my oldest brother, Alan, my best friend Vanessa then my other brother Danny—in that order. Vanessa was going to drive to the house and get me but I could not wait. I drove to the hospital in a daze where staff took me to that damn sitting area. A room located near the Intensive Care Unit (ICU) set apart from everyone else. A place I had been once before with a friend who had lost her mom. I knew that is the room where you went when there was no hope. It was the "it is over" room. No more wishing, hoping or prayers. The your-life-will- never-be-the-same room. The dreaded life changing room. It was done, my fifty-three-year-young husband of close to sixteen years was gone. My mind flashed back to the man I shared vows with. The words, "To death do you part," hit me like a brick wall being thrown through a window and breaking it into pieces, but the window was my heart.

Eventually, I left the change room. A doctor led me to where his body was. I was so grateful to go back and see him. I guess I was hoping to find him alive. That it had all been a horrible mistake. That he was ok but it was not a mistake. He was at peace. His body was done with this time on earth and his spirit was just beginning. For me, he was the body that I could touch, feel, see and hear. Now he was spirit that I could not touch, feel, hear or see. Not that night. He was a shell I had to say goodbye to. His body was empty, but his spirit was full.

I had to go home. I had to call my son and tell him his step-dad was gone. Robert called Mark dad who was like a father to him. He had been with Robert since he was two and a half years old. Robert was hundreds of miles away and only six months into his Navy career. He was about to receive the phone call no son wants to get, especially at such a young age. I said, "Robert, Mark is gone." He said, "Mom, are you sure? I think you need to check with the doctors. Mom, you just think that." Miles away, a cold phone call and a familiar voice echoed very foreign words. His dad had died.

Thus the changes began. Just like that. In one day. One run. One life gone. How could it be?

I wanted to stay in that cold hospital room. I longed to stay with the empty shell that lay in those white sheets. I wanted to cuddle with him, to feel his arms around me, hear his voice and see his blue eyes. The body that once had life, laughter, smiles, tears, anger and pain was a shell now. I felt inclined to stay until the nightmare was over. And when I woke up everything would be like it was before Mark went for his run.

But I had to leave. I had to do what I heard other people did when they lost their loved ones: make arrangements. That seems funny— arrangements for whom? For what? What was to be arranged—my life? My son's life? The funeral, the paddle-out? Letting friends know they had lost Mark? Arranging what, for God's sake? My life had just *been* arranged to something I could not bear. Life without Mark. I did not want to arrange anymore. I wanted to rearrange everything to the way it was before Mark's run. Could we not just rearrange?

Labor Pains

Photo Credit: August Perry

Mark, it has been one week since you went to your real home. It seems like it is still that night…last Monday…when they told me you were gone. I still cannot believe you are not here. I cannot grasp it at all. But you are at your real home. Even though I know you are ok, and my world has stopped. Time has stood still and I am not sure when it will begin again.

Paul's letters in the Bible tells us to live is Christ and to die is gain. You did just that: You lived for Him and now you have gained Him. You are with your love. I am left here to carry on for whatever purpose.

Mark, it hurts so bad. It is like labor pains that come in waves. But the pain is like waves inside my heart breaking over and over again. The pain comes faster and faster with no relief and no epidural to ease them. No birth from these pains...only the thought when will it ease up. The only relief I have is knowing I will see you again and that you are so full of joy right now. It is just like the relief that comes when your child is born. The physical pain ends and the joy begins. Your birth came again... heaven...Mark...I love you...I miss you.

"Let not your hearts be troubled. Believe in God; Believe in Jesus. In my Father's house are many rooms. If it were not so, would I have told you that I go to prepare a place for you? And if I go and prepare a place for you, I will come again and will take you to myself, that where I am you may be also. And you know the way to where I am going" (John 14:1–2).

Sucked Down a Dark Hole.

"She was overstrained with grief and loneliness; almost any shoulder would have done as well." —F. Scott Fitzgerald

Mark, today has been two weeks. You know, honey, I have been running as fast as I can. I have been trying to escape the reality that you are in a prepared home in heaven and I am still here. The shock began to leave me when I hit that wall—no, when I smashed into that wall. It was as if my heart and body had been broken into several tiny pieces scattered all over the place. I mean they are everywhere. Pieces. I could never even find them, much less figure out how to put them back together. A whole heart or a whole body. I wonder how Jesus is going to pick the pieces up and put them back together. I cannot. I would not even know where to begin.

Grief is a lonely place. It is as if I have been sucked down a hole that I do not want to be in. It is dark and I do not know where the end is. I fight it. I fight it because I do not want to be in this dark hole. But here I am. I am here whether I fight it or not. The suction from the darkness keeps me there. There is no light and there are no people. I would rather my life be like it was, Mark, when you were here. But it is not and it will never be again.

Mark, we have all these great friends. Your friends have been so sweet to me. You have the best friends, Mark. They loved you so much and I have the best friends too. We are so blessed. That being said, I still feel so terribly alone. Most of the time no one really knows what to do or say. How can they? I do not even know what to do or say. I want to talk but I don't. I want to hug someone but I don't. I want a friend but I want you. No one can enter this place with me—no one but Jesus. Everyone tells me that it will get better with each passing day. They try to say the right thing. Mark, I miss you more with each passing day and it presently seems that it will keep getting worse. I love you so much and need your direction in so many areas of my life but you are not here. Honey, I pray that through your death the Lord will be glorified and I will honor you. Peace. I need Peace.

"Trust in the Lord with all your heart, and do not lean on your own understanding. In all your ways acknowledge him, and he will make straight your paths" (Prov. 3:5–6).

The Rollercoaster

"No one ever told me that grief felt so like fear."
—C.S. Lewis

It has been three weeks since you went home. On one hand, it seems as if time has stood still. I cling to you and I do not want to let you go. On the other hand, it seems as if it has been eternity since I last saw your face, felt your touch or heard your laugh. I can see there are no shortcuts around this grief. I would love for there to be one. I am not good at this sort of thing. I do not have a lot of patience with myself. I would rather skip, jump over, go around or ignore the journey to healing.

My emotions are on a rollercoaster ride. I wish they would take the merry-go–round. A merry-go-round is always pacifying. I used to like the roller-coaster ride. I used to like the thrill of being scared on rides and feeling that fear. Remember when we rode the roller-coaster in Myrtle Beach acting like kids? We rode the merry-go-round as well and many times with Robert. Robert never liked the roller-coaster when he was little but he loved the merry-go-round. What has happened to the merry-go-round? I do not want to feel this fear anymore. There is no comfort from this fear or is there?

"But we do not want you to be uniformed brothers, about those who are asleep, that you may not grieve as others do who have no hope."
—1Thessalonians 4:13

The Identity

I still do not feel like doing anything. My mind has to make my feet move forward. Family and friends have been supportive. And, well, Jesus…life is not worth living without Him. I know that when I pray to Jesus, you are right there, Mark, looking at Jesus. Wow…Jesus connects me to you. I like that connection. I do not understand any of this but I do not have to. I only have to trust Jesus. It is what gets me through.

Because…it would be so easy to use grief as my identity. My mind keeps telling my heart, "Don't put the grief identity on and do not wear that label." So when I read the following from *Grieving with Hope,* it rang true:

As you are trying to adjust to your new reality, be careful not to choose grief as your new identity. Your grief and your loss should never define you. As Paul Tripp says, "Grief is a very significant human experience. It was never meant to be an identity. When I take it on as an identity, it will hurt me."

If you take on grief as your identity, you will give yourself permission to isolate yourself, sleep away the days, let your responsibilities go, ignore your family—all the while telling yourself, 'It's okay because I'm grieving'…

Grief is not an identity, and if I make it my identity, I will start giving way to the definition of that identity I have given it. Grief is a profound experience to go through and it rocks a person to the core.

It is disruptive, dislocating and highly emotional. But this experience does not define me. Christ defines me.[1]

The questions I'm asking myself now are: What identity am I putting on? What label am I wearing? Maybe, I want to wear my grief identity. Maybe I want to get up every day and put this label on. It is defining me and I hate it. I hate it. I cannot get it off. It is sewn on.

Ticket for the
Next Train . . . Please

"The darker the night, the brighter the stars,
the deeper the grief the closer God."
—*Fyodor Dostoyevsky*

Well, Mark, I am walking into my fourth week since you went home. Four weeks. Maybe it is more like stumbling into my first month without you by my side. Strange times. I have true empathy for those who lose loved ones and I think about those who suffer losing more than one person at a time or over a short period. I cannot imagine it. I cannot fathom their pain. I cannot even fathom mine.

The grief at times is almost more than I can endure. I wanted to hop on a train the other night and go…somewhere other than here. Anywhere

---

[1] Samuel J. Hodges IV and Kathy Leonard, *Grieving with Hope: Finding Comfort as You Journey Through Loss* (Grand Rapids, MI: Baker Books, 2011), 53 and 54.

fast would be good…faster…farther. To *nowhere* would be good. Away from the memories of you and I. To a place I could just erase everything that was happening. To a place that everything would be like it was. Away from this sorrow.

Part of me is gone… I cannot run from that. You went your way and now I have to go mine. I have to face it. When will I believe you are really gone? You know my mind knows you are not coming back but in my heart there is hope.

I took all your clothes and things out of the room. Someone said it was too soon. I said, "I can look at those things for a year and it would not bring Mark back." I can smell them, wear them or treasure them. However, Mark, you are not physically in the clothes or memories. You are not here. I look for you but you are not here.

I cannot seem to even find a picture of you that is any good. Because the picture is just a memory. I want to hear your voice, hear your laugh, see your face move…The photograph does not have your varying facial expressions or your laughter.

I am thankful for the times we did have together, Mark. I am thankful for the blessings that have come in the midst of this pain. Peace and suffering, blessings and tragedies—they can be bound together as one.

My mind cannot fathom the depth of love You have for us, Jesus, or what You suffered on that forsaken cross. You, above all, know what suffering is about—what pain, loss and abandonment are. You and You alone can enter my pain. No one else can walk with me during this time in the potter's hand. I really would not want anyone to try. Because they can't. After all, Jesus, you created me. You know what is in my heart more than I do. You died for me, for us—who else has ever died so I could live again? That I can see Mark again.

"Then I saw a new heaven and a new earth, for the first heaven and the first earth had passed away, and the sea was no more. And I saw the Holy City, new Jerusalem, coming down out of heaven from God, prepared as a bride adorned for her husband. And I heard a loud voice from the throne saying, 'Behold, the dxwelling place of God is with man. He will dwell with them as their God. He will wipe away every tear from their eyes, and death shall be no more, neither shall there be mourning nor crying nor pain anymore, for the former things had passed away'" — Revelations 21:1–4.

Lord, may I be a light for You today.

Valentine's Day

In a letter to Thomas Jefferson on May 6, 1816, John Adams wrote, "Grief drives men into the habits of serious reflection, sharpens the understanding, and softens the heart."[2]

I made it through another week of this process called mourning. I have to admit, last week was one of the toughest yet. Valentine's Day was almost more than I could bear. A friend came by and brought me flowers. She meant nothing but love and care. But for me it was a stark reminder that you, honey, were not there to give me flowers as you always did. I told her thank you very quickly and practically slammed the door in her face. I thought the nerve of her to remind me of my husband's absence on Valentine's day. That is what happens when you lose your sense of thankfulness at times. You lose who you are. You forget who your friends

---

[2] John Adams, *The Works of John Adams, Second President of the United States, Volume 10* (Boston: Little, Brown and Company, 1856), 218.

and enemies are. My friends are not the enemy…the enemy is fear. This Valentines it sure did not seem like my friend was a friend. Valentine's Day was so special to us. We had even bought these champagne flutes from Waterford Chrystal that had hearts on them just for Valentines. I thought Mark and I would be toasting good cheer with them again this year but instead I was toasting my grief. I did allow Jesus in after I slid down the wall with flowers in hand wirh familiar tears running down my cheeks.

Another way to express this first holiday without Mark…through anger and tears. I emerged from under the weight of the crushing waves that held me under, taking my breath, making me feel as if my lungs would burst from lack of air and tossing me around as I looked for the surface.

I was only stronger after Valentines was over when Jesus reached down and rescued me from drowning. So much so which gave me a more intimate look at Jesus. I promise you, I could reach out and touch His face. I think of Peter wanting to walk on water. Then sinking. Jesus immediately—yes, immediately—reached out His hand and pulled him up. "O you of little faith, why did you doubt?" (Matt. 14:31). Why *do* we doubt? Why do we doubt that Jesus will rescue us? Why do we doubt His word?

Regret

"Grief is not as heavy as guilt, but it takes more away from you."
—Veronica Roth

Ever want a memory to be real? Ever want reality just to be an illusion? Ever want the dream back? It just seems like too much work to begin again. Sometimes it feels like I do not have the energy to have a new dream. The old dream was once that new dream. The new hope of a wonderful life.

This morning was one of those mornings when I wish my reality was…well…not my reality.

I was tucking away some more pictures and admiring Mark's signed surfboard last night. Everyone had signed his surfboard at the celebration of life and paddle out. Mark loved that board. He was a keeper and took great care of those things he treasured. He did not have one mark on that board and it was thirty- four years old. I will never forget the morning I looked at it and panicked when I saw all the signatures. For one small second…I thought Mark is going to kill me. That second between hope and reality. So? I was just doing one step at a time to help the reality not be hope that he was still here somewhere. It was therapeutic going through some things of his…sorting…putting away. My way.

Looking at his surfboard made me flash back to an image in my mind. A memory of a dream that was lost and full of regret.

Regret: Sorrow caused by something beyond one's power to remedy.

I generally look at past experiences as learning, growing and molding experiences. In other words, I am one who would say, "I have no regrets in life." Even though…there is plenty of my life that I would like to have not occurred. Through the years, I have learned that those choices and experiences, even the ones I had absolutely no control over or did not like have made me who I am—strong, a survivor and a lover of life and of others.

However, there is one regret that keeps haunting me. It is the regret of only surfing with Mark three times in the Fall one year. For over seventeen years he wanted me to surf with him. I did not. I do not know why I chose not to. I enjoyed watching him and being a small part of that community (which at the time I never really understood)

17

It was two summers ago when Mark got me out in the water at the end of August. A good friend of Mark's let me ride his board. It was a nine-foot longboard. His buddies Herb and Garrett (he took Garrett under his wing. He just loved him and wanted to help him become a better surfer . . .which he has—Mark would be so proud). Mark was so proud of me. He said I stood on the first wave and rode the line. I did not know what that was, but hey—Mark loved it!

In fact, while going through his messages on Facebook, after he died, I saw where he told a friend about it—about how excited he was that I went out surfing. He said he could not wait until the next summer when I could surf again—and said how proud he was of me.

But I did not surf that summer, the summer of 2011. I was too busy working on my personal training, coaching studies and certifications because I needed to start working again.

Then he died that January. Wow…regrets.

So…when he died, I was trying to line up a canoe or something I could go out in for the paddle-out…so I could spread his ashes. Morning came and I was crouching by our favorite brown chair. The one in which I write now, by the sliding glass door through which I could see the ocean and the cabanas. As I kneeled there, I said to God, "I don't want to live anymore. I cannot live without Mark. I do not want to live without Mark. Please take me. Why didn't you take me instead of Mark?"

Anyway, I had planned to get someone to canoe me out at the paddle-out because I had only surfed once two summers previously. A complete total of just three times. Of all days I did not feel like it. Then, as I was asking God to take me, telling Him I did not want to live, I heard Him say, "GET UP. You are not dead. You are ALIVE and well with a purpose. Look around." I looked through the sliding glass door at all of Mark's friends waving at me from the beach getting the paddle-out. It was life. Everyone was living life. Celebrating Mark's life. Remembering their good times with him. I was among the living. As numb as I felt, I was still alive. I had not died with Mark. His purpose was done. My purpose was not and neither were those of the others who still lived.

God is good like that, you know—supplying what you need at the very moment you need it. When you are broken, He sends love, grace, goodness, friends and family your way.

Well, it was like I had this sudden strength...like Jesus was compelling me—like Mark was compelling me—to paddle out on a board. So, someone called Herb and he brought the board I had used a couple of summers ago. I am paddling out. I am not canoeing out. . . That's not who I am. I am Sweet Strength! That is what Mark told me. I paddled out on that board: energy high, love deep and a spirit driven to honor my best friend. And I was not even cold.

Since that day, I have felt compelled to be in the water...to have that oneness with God, with Mark and with friends.

But I still have that regret that I cannot surf with the one person who loved it most and who wanted me to surf with him. He would be so proud of me and probably would not believe I was out there in that cold water. I would give anything for the opportunity to surf with Mark...to be with him in that water. I may not be that good...yet...but I *will* get better because I am determined. I know that Mark would want me to continue to live life and not have regrets, even of not going out surfing with him...but I do.

I hope that he is looking over me. Somehow I know he is. Hey, I have his fins on my board—and they're more expensive than the board! Mark would like that.

I love you, Mark. I hope I make you proud in the water. I am sure going to try.

Everywhere, but Nowhere

"Without you in my arms, I feel an emptiness in my soul. I find myself searching the crowds for your face – I know, it's an impossibility, but I cannot help myself." —Nicholas Sparks

I cannot believe that on the ninth it will have been four months since Mark went home. Time has stood still for me in the midst of the movement of the clock. I still find it hard to believe that you are not with me. Mark grew up here and knew so many people, and so many people loved him. We have so many special places we went together…but he simply is not in any of those places.

In fact, I went to one of those places yesterday…our favorite Mexican Restaurant, Fiesta Mexicana, hoping to meet him there. I was with our friends. Surely they knew where you were. I just wanted to be around who Mark was around, who loved him, who he loved. I wanted to go to our usual spots, hoping to grab a glimpse of him. I even turned my car around the other day to go back and get a better look at a bicyclist I had passed who looked just like you bud. I know it seems so crazy. I see you in the lineup in the water with the surfers. I could swear I see you. The guy on the bike had your grey hair, your smile and a surf shirt on. Mark is everywhere but nowhere to be found. Now, I know he is not in any of those special places just like I knew he was not on that bike but my heart just wanted him to be there so badly. So yesterday was a special day of grieving, which is good. It is okay to grieve, to cry, to miss Mark…in fact, it is very healing. I thought it would be easier by now but it is not. I am beginning to wonder when it will. I know to my friends I must be hard to understand. I am not who I was. I do not even know who I am now.

Everything has changed. I used to love change but this is just too much. Nothing is the same—*nothing*. Every aspect of my life is seen differently and has all changed to me! However, the physical appearances of objects and people such as where I live, the pictures I have hanging, the position of furniture, my family and friends, the sunrises and sunsets and my daily routine all appear on the outside normal as before. Because I see through a different lens. A lens that I can never seem to focus through. Yes, change is everywhere to me.

Earlier today, as I listed all the changes in my mind, wishing there was *something* in my life that had not changed. I heard this strong but faint voice say to me, "Linda…I have not changed. I am the same yesterday, today and tomorrow. I will never change. I am alpha and omega, beginning and end. I will neither leave nor forsake you. When your heart and flesh fail, I will be your strength forever. What a relief that was for me—a comfort—to hear that voice and to know there is *something* I can count on that does not change: God. He is always with us…always pulling for us, loving us and comforting us. He is the lone rock in the midst of sinking sand. As we change and things around us change we can count on the one who never changes. He will not let you go. There are two things you can count on in this life: Your life will change but God will not.

God, I pray for all those who are dealing with change in their lives. For those who are thinking, *this is just too much change; it's too hard*—God. I pray that You will remind them that you are God who does not change. You will bless and keep them and will make your face shine upon them. I pray that they will be granted the grace and love to see you clearly. I pray that they will see that You are their hope and comfort in this ever changing world in which we live.

No Dinner

"So it's true when all is said and done, grief is the price we pay for love"
—*E.A. Bucchianeri*

Mark, I would love to wake up this morning and say, "Happy anniversary! With God I look forward to more years together. You are home and I am here. No flowers, no three card, and no dinner at our favorite restaurant today, not this year. I remember our fifth anniversary date. You always made anniversaries so special. We went to Greg Normans Grill in North Myrtle Beach. You pulled out this little black case. You handed it to me and said "Happy Anniversary!" I opened it up. It was the most beautiful diamond I had ever seen. I could not believe it. I said, "Mark, where did you get this?" He said, "It was in my safe deposit box. It was my great aunt's ring and she gave it to my mom. It was made in 1895." I then jokily said, "What else is in that safe deposit box." I knew at that moment Mark McDandel loved me. He treasured his family's heirlooms. I knew that if he gave me his mom's ring, he deeply loved me. Mark had lost his mom and dad. He was an only child. His dad was an only child. His mom just had one brother. I never understood that about heirlooms. How important they were when you lose someone. I was the one who always cleaned out and threw away. Mark used to pick on me and tell me he was glad I was not the one who found the Dead Sea Scrolls because I would have said, "Look at this old thing, let's toss it." I was never a keeper until now. I do not want to give anything away.

I miss you so much. Part of me is gone, tossed aside and thrown away. But I know you would want me to carry on with my life. I am trying to do just that: learn to live without you, learn a new way. Thank you for living out our marriage vows. I remember the dreams I had the week before you died. I dreamed every night you were leaving me. Leaving me for another lover. I remember picking on you when I would wake up about it. We laughed because I never had to worry about you lying to me, running around on me or leaving me—until now, that is. It is as if the dream was preparing me for your leaving. You did leave me for another lover. You left me for a better life…a better love. Your true love, Jesus, and that makes me smile. Bud, I will always love you. I am so honored to have been your wife. You are gone but babe you are not forgotten. It was for better or worse, richer or poorer and in health and sickness that we made it…until death do us part. I honor you this day…in love.

The World Keeps Spinning

"No matter how bad your heart is broken;
the world doesn't stop for your grief."
— Faraaz Kuzi

I was reading an article on grief and in it the author talks about losing his wife and how the world is still going on around him. Boy, do I relate to him when he says something like this, "Those people don't even know that Cindy's dead, I thought. For them it's business as usual…just like any other day. The world is staying right on schedule and all of life is moving on. How can it be? It doesn't seem right. I felt like crying out, 'Hey folks, don't you know my wife died?

Isn't it written all over my face? My world has crashed, and you don't even care!'"

He goes on to say God gave him a crystal clear message: "Ike, all of this life around you isn't going to stop. It's up to you to decide how much time you will take out of your life before you pick yourself up and go on. You can take a month, three months, six…a year. Or you can take a lifetime. What will it be?"

I like that because it is truth. The world never stops because of our pains or trials, it keeps spinning and people keep living and going about their lives. I could so relate. My world had stopped but no one else's life had stopped. I wanted to scream out loud so many days and say…the same thing…just the name was Mark… he is dead can't you understand that? We however, do have a choice to either join life again or walk out of life. Death happens to everyone although we are never ready for it to happen to us or those we love. One thing is for certain: We are all going to die. We live in a tough world and we aren't promised a rose garden. As Lynn Anderson's song, "Rose Garden," says. When these things happen to us we can choose to linger there or search for the answers to some pivotal questions while we are there. This way we can become stronger and help others as we move forward and out of that feeling of hopelessness and helplessness. We can start living again. It is just some days I want the world to stop with me. Thank you God that you are the one who keeps the world spinning even if I want it to stop.

My Home

"Deep grief sometimes is almost like a specific location, a coordinate on a map of time. When you are standing in that forest of sorrow, you cannot imagine that you could ever find your way to a better place. But if someone can assure you that they themselves have stood in that same place, and now have moved on, sometimes this will bring hope."
— *Elizabeth Gilbert*

Wow, seven months have gone by so quickly as I sifted through the debris in my life…the fallout…the change. Debris always comes with a fallout and then sorting through it all: the treasures and the trash. The death of a loved one and all the trash and treasures that come with it. There are times when the memories seem so haunting that I want an escape and yet there are days they can be so comforting that I want to engrave them in my mind…brand them there so they are seared forever, never to leave.

There are days when I feel like I am on the non-threatening merry-go-round. Round…round…and round we go. It is the same scene…not going anywhere but always moving. Then there are days when I feel I am on a runaway horse that is weary to get back home…racing, fast and furious, to that old familiar place he knows as home. I try to guide him but realize I have absolutely no control. I hold on to the reins, hoping to stop him but all the while praying he will take me home with him to somewhere familiar and comforting. My arms are burning from the grip and my legs are gripping so tightly that they have become numb. Part of me is fearful but another part is excited about the freedom of not knowing where we are headed. I know he knows the way home and all I have to do is not lose my grip. If I hold on tight he will take me home. To the familiar. To safety. To security.

Pain…change…loss…distraction. Please distract me from this loss. Seven months closing in…seven months of finding my way…losing my way…wondering where home is…missing my family, my home. Missing who I was as a wife, all the while moving forward to embrace this new single way of life. Missing my only son, Robert, who is in the Navy now. Missing our family life. Embracing a new life and living it the best I can because I love life. Trying to figure out who this new person is and how I got here and where the heck I am going. Where is my horse that knows the way…that is going to take me home? It is as if I am observing myself from another place and time. Then there is the solid rock I always try to stand on but sometimes in the midst of shifting sand, I lose my balance and fall. Jesus is so aware of where I stand or fall. I know He is with me in my heart and in my soul but honestly there are days when I want Him here in human form not just in spirit form. I long for that embrace. I long for that shoulder to cry and embrace a human touch. Jesus I need your touch.

Why cry? There is no one here. I can almost go into that place Pink Floyd so eloquently sings about. I have become comfortably numb. I think after you have experienced so many changes in your life, year after year— big changes and small—you begin to live differently. You realize that nothing is secure. Earth is not our home. We are truly strangers in this place and time. We really own nothing, and tomorrow could bring another change.

There are days when I say to my friends, "I really want some stability. I need stability." But God says, "I am stability. . . I am all the stability you need." Can I trust that? Do I have a choice? Stability…what is it? Are any of us so sure we have it? When everything is so unsure, it is faith, truth and love that will bring you through.

This is not our home nor our destination. Our journey's end is where we will again meet those we have lost. In the meantime, let us heal, live a life to the fullest and love those who are still with us because those who have gone before us are just fine. Their horse took them home. They do not need us anymore. Faith is the confidence of things hoped for and the conviction of things not seen.

Memories Rewritten

*"When a relationship of love is disrupted, the relationship does not cease.
The love continues; therefore, the relationship continues. The work of grief is
to reconcile and redeem life to a different love relationship."*
— W. Scott Lineberry

Memories etched and memories rewritten. Eight months today. I miss you, honey. Thank you for the words this morning.

About once a month, I like to look at cards Mark gave me and sometimes I look at messages he sent people through Facebook. The following was written about a month before he died. What a special gift to leave with me. He was talking with a friend whom he evidently had not seen in a while.

"I had a heart attack in May 2007 and it is a miracle I am here. However, the Lord saved me that day. I had 100 percent blockage in the 'widow maker' artery, and 97 percent of people don't make it through that. I was under a lot of stress at the time, developing some condos. My family also has a history of heart disease. But I'm doing great now! I'm eating healthy, running, walking, bicycling, and, of course, surfing. The economy did have an effect on me financially, but everything is okay, and I'm married to a wonderful, beautiful woman who stuck with me through all of it."

How could a girl not smile after reading those beautiful words? I am no expert on relationships but I do know that any day could be your last to spend with your partner, friend or family member. With that being said, is it really worth arguing over who took out the trash, or who was supposed to drive the kids to school, or who wronged the other?

Going back to memories, at night there are times when I am lying in bed feeling the darkness, loneliness and the dreaded deafening silence. I think silence is an oxymoron because it can be so loud. Maybe some of you know it...the silence of loneliness. The thoughts of memories reverberating with a sound that becomes etched in the recesses of your mind. You can hear the sounds of the memories. You can see the images so clearly that they become like a tattoo you got in a drunken stupor and now you want to get rid of it. But it is there, etched on your skin, with the sounds surrounding the whole thing. A reminder...a reminder of a night you wish you could erase. Maybe the silence is the lack of that other breath that used to be beside you in the darkness of the night. It felt safe hearing that breath. If you listen closely enough you might be able to hear it.

What a difference the meaning of breathing and breath have on me today. At times there are memories you never want to forget and you try to bring the good memories to life. You squint your eyes so hard and squeeze your teeth together in hope that you can bring the memory of the one you lost back to life. Maybe if I squeeze my eyes together hard enough and think hard enough, I can bring Mark's touch to me. Be able to hear his breath beside me, feel his eyes penetrating my very soul, see his smile, hear his voice and feel his love. Then there is the horrid memory—the one you wish you could forget. The memory of hearing his body hit the kitchen floor, the haunting image of his body in convulsions. The stillness. The stillness of his body as I tried to breathe life back into it. While I hoped that God would come down and breathe for him I knew He could if He wanted to. That is something you can never forget. In fact, it is so loud it sometimes drowns out those memories you want at the forefront of your mind. You cannot just turn the noise down or off it always keeps your mind wide awake and sleep never comes.

This morning during my run I began to see that memory differently on this eight-month path to healing and peace. Peace does come. You can rewrite that memory and it can take the place of the once haunting night, making it beautiful in its own way. Rewriting your story, kind of like lasering off that old tattoo and putting something new in its place. I thought to myself this morning, I am going to rewrite that memory. Yes, it will be erased and rewritten into a beautiful story. A story which is right and true.

As I was trying to breathe life into Mark, Jesus was breathing a new life into Mark. A better breath and a better life than I could ever have given him. His home, his better home. A home that was his real home. Where the beauty is found in death. I got to be with Mark as he breathed his last breath with me and as Jesus gave him his first breath of his new life and his true love. That is reality, truth and that is like a breath of fresh air in a gentle wind. The sound of that memory is like my favorite place: the ocean and the lullaby of the waves crashing onto the shore.

I can now see Mark's lifeless and hollow body on the floor as a beautiful beginning of an everlasting life for Mark.

Mark, I thank you for giving me love. Jesus,

I thank You for allowing me to rewrite my memory so I can see it for what it really is—life, not death.

Encourage

"Maybe everyone can live beyond what they are capable of."
— Markus Zusak

On this cool cloudy morning, I am missing you, Mark. Grief is like that. It just has no rhyme or reason. It is no particular anniversary, holiday, or birthday. It is a day like any other and yet I am struggling with my grief. But I just have to go with it...

In Loving Memory of my Husband and Best Friend, Mark "the Shark"
November 13, 1958 - January 9, 2012

In 1995, I met Mark. I had just divorced and was the mother of a two-and-a-half-year-old. Mark and I fell in love and were married in 1996. We bought our dream home in 1997 and lived our lives to the fullest. Like most married couples, we had our ups and downs but we both chased our own careers. Mark had a couple of different adventures, but he decided he was going to develop at that time condos because the real estate market was booming. Mark put his heart and soul into developing condos. Robert, our son, was enjoying his childhood in an awesome neighborhood, doing what boys love to do best when they live at the ocean. He enjoyed surfing and hanging out with his friends while investigating life.

Meanwhile, my husband was wrapped up in the process of building and trying to sell condos when the market slowed. There were several challenges that arose in the process of building these condos and I could see my husband's stress level rise. We put both our house and the condo on the market and neither ended up selling. But, Mark would smile in the midst of it.

Mark, I miss your smile more than anything. On my run this morning, I was thinking how you would say, "Whoa, doggie mama," when I came out of the bedroom dressed to go out to dinner or somewhere special. You gave me that grin and that look only you could give. You gave me that same grin and look the night before your last run. The day you went home. I will never forget it that day.

Mark always encouraged me and built me up by telling me I was smart and beautiful. That I could do anything I wanted. He mentioned that if anything ever happened to him, I would be fine and to move forward. His words enabled me to take a class for life coaching two weeks after he left me. That encouragement and strength has enabled me, even in the pain, to smile and try to encourage others. His encouragement over the years has allowed me to grow, love who I am and love others where they presently are.

Mark always had a certain smile. He cared for others and wanted them to feel encouraged and like they were his best friend. No one but me ever knew how stressed he was and how he hated what he was dealing with financially all the debt. Mark and I never liked self-pity. It can be fun for a time but there are so many people worse off than you. There are people who have been through or are going through incredibly tough times. All you have to do is walk out your door and look around, read the paper or just look on Facebook. Now, I am not saying you should ignore what you are going through because there are others worse off but know there are also others in a better place than you.

At times encouraging others helps yourself heal. It is okay to grieve, to feel pain and to be in a bad place. You just do not have to stay in that place. There is always a choice and only you can make that choice. I would rather smile and encourage than stay in grief. Mark would want that. He would smile.

In all of this, I am trying to encourage people to love, to laugh and encourage one another in their relationships. To give each other strength so if something happens to one person, the other will be able to move forward and not to have regrets.

I am going to share my smile today…Mark would like that.

Displaced

I am sitting here thinking about the rolling out of the ninth month and heading to the tenth month since Mark went home. I have been pondering about what is now a recurring feeling still trying to identify words that could describe what I am feeling. The words displaced, misplaced and missing could sum up and describe my journey thus far. Kind of like a puzzle that has not been put together yet. I have been trying to figure out the theme or one word that could describe my journey and for me it is the word "displaced." Displaced is best described as being moved from a normal place or position. The dictionary describes the words change and disarranged as the state of being displaced, of having been moved from the usual or proper place. Maybe it is similar to misplaced. Yes, that is how I feel displaced and misplaced. But in the middle of displacement I must learn how to live life again. How to use my displacement as a bridge to learning how to live in my new arranged and disarranged life. Maybe I feel displaced because part of me is missing. Not necessarily the physical aspect of feeling like I do not have a home but the heart of it. Yes, my heart is displaced partially because I am not home yet, my real home. I mean we are all going to die.

Death happens every day and you never know when your time will be. That is why it is so important to live each day with a purpose as Mark, lived each day loving Jesus and others. Today I will live, love and weep for those I miss. Mark's death lives on in glory and has been resurrected. However, losing him feels like his death is a part of me. I know Jesus will sustain me because that is His promise I will see you again Mark. The displacement will be gone and I will be home. It's okay for now to feel displaced. It somehow makes you search for life.

"Can one be fully human without experiencing tragedy?...The only tragedy there is in the world is not awake and unawareness. From them comes fear, and from fear comes everything else, but death is not a tragedy at all. Dying is wonderful; it's only horrible to people who have never understood life. It's only when you're afraid of life that you fear death. It's only dead people who fear death...The end of the world for a caterpillar is a butterfly for the master."[3]

Pushing Yourself

This morning I woke up really missing Mark. Grief had found me once again. It was one of those mornings when I just wept for the loss, the closeness, the love, the hugs, snuggles, and smiles, the smell of his coffee brewing and the sound of him breathing beside me. My heart aches. Like

---

[3] Anthony de Mello, *Awareness: The Perils and Opportunities of Reality (Colorado Springs: Image Books, 2003), 150.*

Bruce Springsteen sings, "Sometimes it's like someone took a knife, baby, edgy and dull, and cut a six-inch valley through the middle of my soul." That pretty much sums it up.

I guess with Mark's birthday on the horizon and the one-year anniversary of him going home being a couple of months away, it is really hard.

How do I even manage to get going on this cloudy, cold day? I am not much of a cold-weather person. In fact, the thought of moving to some warm tropical island is very tempting but I am here for a while. I might as well embrace the fact that winter is coming and enjoy it. I could complain about the weather and hate it but that would not make it go away. It certainly would not make me any happier. I have decided to somehow embrace this.

This morning when I pushed myself to get out and run it felt so refreshing and exhilarating. I felt great. I am alive and still here for a purpose. Making yourself do those things you do not always feel like doing is how you begin to change, to grow and to break through those invisible barriers that try to crush you and keep you down. The feeling of doing it is so much stronger than not doing it…not moving…not growing…not stretching. I want to live and live life to the fullest, until it is my turn to go home. Life is so short.

Mark would want me too.

I knew I could keep crying or I could do what has kept me going and moving forward through this grieving process—running on the beach, surfing, learning new things, exercising, eating healthy, keeping my mind positive, praying and building my business of helping others. *I love to help others.* All of these experiences build my strength. It is how I manage to walk through this incredible pain with laughter, love, fun and a positive view of life.

Runner's High

"The gift of grief is that it presents us with the
opportunity to heal and grow." —Jewish Proverb

Ever heard of 'runner's high'? That's no myth—your body rewards exercise by releasing endorphins (the feel-good hormone). It is more than just the temporary feeling that well being 'runner's high' brings. Exercise has proven very effective in relieving symptoms of mental health conditions like anxiety, seasonal affective disorder and clinical depression. New research shows thirty to sixty minutes of daily exercise to be as effective as antidepressant medication in the treatment of mood disorders. If team sports are your thing, they add yet another dimension to the mental wellness effects of activity. The social benefits of combining activity and teamwork are undeniable.

"Exercise reactivates your mind-body connection, putting you back in touch with your creativity and problem-solving abilities, ultimately improving mental clarity. So go ahead: Write yourself a prescription for exercise and banish your winter blues or creative blockages for good!"[4]

Yesterday, my gynecologist and I were talking about how I was handling my grief and how much exercise and eating healthy helps combat depression. Not only does a lack of exercise and poor nutrition affect our health but also on our emotions and our minds.

Depression is real. Depression is something that I battled for a few years. But with prayer, exercise, healthy eating and keeping my mind and

---

[4] Brendan Brazier, "How to Use Fitness to Create Mental and Physical Strength for Life Part 2," *Shanghai Veggie Club, December 30, 2012, http://www.shanghaivegetarians.com/veganfitness-with-brendan-brazier-activity-how-to-use-fitness-to-create-mental-and-physicalstrength-for-life-part-2/.*

thoughts positive I know that I can do anything. You are the only one holding yourself back. Learning to look at yourself outside of yourself, from a non-judgmental view is one of the best things you can do. As Friedrich Nietzsche said, "One's own self is well hidden from one's own self; of all mines of treasure, one's own is the last to be dug up."

Love Bigger Than Anger

"Anger is the result of love. It is energy for defense of something you love when it is threatened." —Tim Keller

I am optimistic, motivational and full of life. A weight was lifted off of me this morning. I didn't even know it was there until it was lifted. Wow.

Jesus is *love*…and He loves, even when we cannot. I did not think I would be angry during this grieving process. Because I love Jesus so much, I did not think I would ever get angry at Him. My faith is strong but this month I have been angry. Sunday night was the height of that anger and self-pity was running a close second. I believe they go hand-in-hand: anger and self-pity or anger and pride. It is hard to be full of love and anger at the same time. It is hard to be humble and angry as well.

I wonder if I will ever be the same. Two weeks ago, I hurt my arm skiing. I was missing my family, missing Mark and the silence was too much to bear. My financial state was rocky and everything seemed to be crashing down on me. Physical pain, emotional pain—it felt good, actually, to be in physical pain…to feel it. I was so mad at God. I said, "Well, you took my husband. You have taken most of my material things. My son is in the Navy. Now I am in pain and cannot continue to surf, workout, water ski or train my clients. Are you happy now? Is this where you wanted me broken?"

Then I heard the Lord say to me, "I am so much bigger than your anger. I love you, and I have plans for you. I will never leave nor forsake you. I know pain, I know loss, I know anger. It's okay to cry. It's okay to be mad. It's okay."

Two days later, the anger was gone.

Courage

"Courage does not always roar. Sometimes it is the quiet voice
at the end of the day saying, 'I will try again tomorrow.'"
—Mary Anne Radmacher

Yesterday, after being interviewed on Donna Tyson's "Rivers of Faith" program, I was feeling pretty good. Talking about my grief and talking about who Mark was helpful. It was encouraging. Having a good day is always refreshing but then I receive this phone call. It was one of those phone calls that throws you this curveball out of nowhere. You are whistling through your day, thinking this is going to be a good day and then something comes out of left field. Anyway, I said to myself, do I not have enough to deal with right now? I want a break. But at the end of the day I pray and give it to God. I say to myself, maybe this or that could happen . . . .. I have to remind myself: Do not react to something that may or may not happen. Today your daily bread has been given. Today, you are fine. Today is a gift. Tomorrow you will get up, put one foot in front of the other, smile, give thanksgiving for another day, point your feet in the direction of that straight path and walk forward. Yes, it is easy to react during grief but it takes courage not too.

Sole Provider, Soul Provider

Sole provider, soul provider. Loneliness lies in the midst of people where there are nights you dread going to sleep. I often lie there with my own thoughts in the dark. The silence of loneliness—what an oxymoron. Loneliness is not really silent. You have these thoughts that reverberate with such a loud sound that you wish they were silent. Maybe silence is the lack of another voice, to be heard in the night when you are alone.

Maybe that is what they mean by silence.

There are days and nights when I feel I do not have a friend in sight. There are days when I feel I have too many to even say hello to. My soul is always crying out. My prayer life seems rather weak right now. I had someone pray for me the other day and I was so thankful. No one has prayed for me in such a long time. Is anyone listening…does anyone listen?

No one gets heard anymore. Everyone is so busy talking over others…trying to get others to hear their side and their story that really, no one is listening. Everyone wants to be right and to be heard. I think that is why there is such loneliness and no one seems to listen. Through all of this, I have learned that the biggest contribution I want to give to others is listening and hugs too. Hugs and listening.

After time, people just go back to their lives, they have to. That is what happens in our world. It keeps on turning. It is funny when people expect you to do certain things or be a certain way. People have all kinds of advice for when you are hurting. Advice for when you are trying to figure it all out but they do not listen.

Loneliness…Jesus knows loneliness. . .and he listens…

Perfect Time

"There is a time for everything and a season for every activity under the heaven: A time to be born and a time to die and a time to plant and a time to uproot." — Ecclesiastes 3:1-2

I have really been reflecting on Mark's death and the timing of it all. Some would say it was an accident and he was too young. Personally, I believe it was God's perfect timing. I believe there are no accidents or coincidences with God. As painful as it is, I truly believe it was perfect. I never really question why God does anything He does. I do not understand everything but I do not question it. I reflect upon it. Death and accidents bring us to a time of reflection. Reflection of our lives and those around us. Isn't that ironic? Death brings us face-to-face with life.

Life suddenly becomes more than the daily trip to Starbucks, the next meeting, the finishing project that is pressing in on us, the petty disagreement with a spouse about who is right and who is wrong or who is going to take the kids to soccer. Time stops. It stands still. All of a sudden, the diaper that needs changing in the middle of a sleepless night becomes about a baby who depends on us for love and care. That friend who wants to chat at the post office when you are in a hurry becomes a chance to take time out of the day to laugh and listen. The sunrise you fail to see in the morning when you are in too big of a hurry or too tired to get up. However, it seems to be the first thing you want to embrace. Life becomes bigger than our minds can wrap around. Time seems to have a time of its own. Time is always clicking, it stops for no one. We realize we can no longer control or manage time. There is someone bigger than time…someone outside our time.

"Your eyes saw my unformed substance; in your book were written, every one of them, the days that were formed for me, when as yet there were none of them" —Psalm. 139:16

As I think about God's timing and reflect on Mark's life, death and his continued life in his real home, I am in awe of our Lord's sovereignty and the preparation He makes in His perfect time. You see, He had been preparing Mark to see Him face-to-face and He had been preparing me for a life without Mark. I see His hand over the last five years in this preparation for us to go our separate ways—together, but for now separate.

In May of 2007, as the market continued to dive, Mark had his first heart attack at the age of forty-eight years old. We had gone to the doctor earlier because he had been complaining of chest pain. The doctor gave him antibiotics and did X-rays. He said Mark had pneumonia and sent him home. Later that night, he was in more pain and wanted me to call the doctor, who recommended going to the ER. Mark did not want to go and stayed up most of the night. By morning he had agreed to go to the hospital.

At the emergency room, Mark started sweating and turned ashen. They took him immediately. He was having a heart attack and needed surgery. It all happened so fast. I immediately prayed, "Lord, I cannot lose him. Please do not take him from me." From the moment we arrived at the emergency room to surgery completion was seventy-seven minutes. The doctor told me Mark had had 100 percent blockage in his main artery, called the widow maker. The doctors all said that it was a miracle he survived. I broke down. I went in to see him where all I saw were the machines he was hooked up to. He had less than 10 percent damage to his heart when they had put in a stent. He was alive and going to be okay.

That is when reality crept in. All the work Mark and I were doing had us going in different directions. Within seventy-seven minutes both of our lives were changed forever. We were connected again like magnets. One of the first questions he asked the doctor was, "Am I going to be able to surf again?" Mark: a child of God and always a surfer. He was on the NSSA team in the early '70s and was the NSSA National Champion in 1978. The doctor said yes! Immediately, Mark was ready to get out of that hospital and put his feet on the familiar feel of his surfboard and be in his favorite spot, the ocean waves. I cannot explain in words the relief and thankfulness I felt in my heart. He was going to be okay.

I told him the next day I would never argue with him or get mad at him again. He smiled and said, "Can I have that in writing?" We both got a big laugh out of it.

We came home and got settled in and I started cooking healthier foods, taking any junk out of the house. His friends joked, "lentils and rice." As I found out later, he snuck in his favorite foods when he would meet the guys out. We were still in the year 2007 and Mark was sure he would get the condos completed and sold. Surely, God was going to relieve him of his financial struggles; after all, he had survived this life-threatening heart attack. But the Lord had other plans because Mark had not fully realized that all he needed was God. God was also preparing me in another way. Mark's heart attack made me think a lot about what I would do if something happened to Mark. It had almost happened. Well, we never got relieved of our financial burdens or of other trials we were to face and overcome in the few years we had left together. Instead, God used those years to strengthen me and to prepare Mark for his time on earth to end. He drew us closer together and our relationships with Jesus grew even stronger, both together and separately.

Mark started using his testimony, his story of near death and of his financial demise as a platform to show what Jesus can do in your life if you depend solely on him for everything. We began realizing that Jesus was working in the little and the big things. We saw His hand on every aspect of our lives and Robert's life. Mark made a comment to me after we had lost our home and the condos, and stated "When we were going through all of that financial loss, you know what God was saying to me? He was saying to me, 'I am all you need, Mark.'"

I often say we really need to have a wide lens on what the Lord is doing instead of a narrow lens that just captures one part of the landscape. It is like a needlepoint underneath the fabric are all these strings mixed and mangled, no rhyme or reason but when you flip it over it is this beautiful work. The Creator sees the big picture. God was giving us testimonies and stories to share, to show how much Jesus loves and cares for us. The Lord even used Mark's death to bring people to Him.

You see, we all have stories and testimonies. It is all about drawing us closer to the one who holds time in His hand. Life is all about God and His story. Jesus reveals Himself through testimony, through the times of happiness, joy, pain and sorrow. It is what the Bible teaches, stories of everyday people who lived life through a time period that holds an eternal time for God.

Maybe time does heal, especially outside of this time, in another place where there will be no pain. I guess I am still being prepared. I have more stories to tell and more testimonies to give. May God bless us with eyes to see His love for us in the midst of our accidents…in the midst of our pain.

Lord, thank You for the wonderful gift of a husband in Mark that you gave me. Thank You for giving us the unique preparation we need to part from this world. Thank You for the fact that no matter what we may be feeling, you never leave nor forsake us.

Celebrating

"Life is like riding a wave. To keep your balance, you must keep moving."
—Eric Carlson

Happy birthday, Mark! It is hard to believe that you are no longer with me. I know you are having a celebration in heaven. I bet it is the best birthday you have ever had. You are with all your family now and I bet you are catching the best waves and eating the best cake. And I know you are getting the best love you have ever received. Wow...I am jealous. I know if you were here, I could not give you all that. I miss you. The grief has been difficult at times but I know you are so much happier where you are, with God. That is what keeps me focused—well, somewhat focused...You know me: go, go, go! Especially now ...even more so now...movement is what gets me through.

You would have celebrated your fifty-fourth birthday with me. I remember us talking about what we would do in our fifties. Well, we did some of it. The tears fall and my heart is so sad. My heart is sad for me, not you, as I think about not being with you for your birthday. What a journey this has been. Mark, I just never knew it would be this hard. But that is life. I am left here for a reason and you are home. It was your time. I do not understand it all but I do not have to. I just trust and know that it will all be okay in the end. Thank you for allowing me to be a part of seventeen years of celebrating your birthdays. Love, cards, dinners, intimacy, fights, makeups, laughs and just dang fun along with crazy years. Happy birthday, bud! You rocked and are rocking on, "Mark the Shark."

And Mark, I am rocking on too and soaking up the sun because of you. You have given me all I need to rock on. Thank you for showing me love so I know what love is. I know what it can be. I will be able to love again! I am going to try and surf on your birthday, today. Hopefully there are waves, catch you in the water!

His Love of Surfing

"I could not help concluding this man had the most supreme pleasure while he was driven so fast and so smoothly by the sea."
—*Captain James Cook*

I just had my two-year breast cancer screening. I am still cancer-free. Thank You, Jesus. That was the longest dang few minutes, waiting for the results. Mark was with me last year. It seemed even longer waiting by myself. But I felt your presence Mark. You know, I remember after my surgery the waves were good. Our little oceanfront condo that a friend let us rent after we lost our home. It was our honeymoon spot. You loved checking the waves out the front door and walking across to surf. This day was no exception. I remember you looking at me and saying, "The waves are great! Do you mind if I go surf, are you okay?" I looked at you and said, "Well now if something happens to you how am I supposed to swim out and get you?" We both laughed. I said, "Go ahead, I will be sleeping anyway." Gosh, I miss you and feeling your love of the water.

Jesus

What is on my mind? Jesus Christ and going into the eleventh month of my grieving process. Comfortably numb, like Pink Floyd's song…that's how the days' end: comfortably numb.

Wow…has it really been almost eleven months? It is hard to wrap my mind around it. On my run this morning, I thought about the last eleven months and having Jesus with me during this journey. You know what I love about Jesus? He knows everything about me. To be honest there is nothing that I can hide from Him. He knows every dark place in my heart, every evil thought, every time I have denied Him and every lie I have told. He knows the sin that I have committed or will commit in the future. He knows every fiber of my being and yet He understands. You know what the miracle is? He still loves me, just as I am…not as I think I should be or as someone else may think I should be. I can talk to Him. I do not have to hide things from Jesus because He knows me so well. He created me. . . He knows my next move. That is the miracle—His love…His love of me. I have never had that kind of love anywhere else before. I relish it. I love the freedom in that: being able to tell Him everything with no condemnation, no judgment—just love. Jesus has been my rock through this grief. Jesus always knows where I am on my journey. . . I do not have to explain it to Him.

Other people, with good intentions, always want to tell you where they think you are on your journey. They base it on their experiences in life. It is hard to separate our experiences when we see others in a similar situation. But with Jesus, there is no trying to convince, no trying to make someone understand.

My prayers through this have gone something like this: Good morning, God, thank you for this day and thank you for looking over my family, friends and me.

Dad's timing

I am a little overwhelmed today. Wishing Mark was here. My dad is dying and we have hospice in. We were going to transfer him from the hospital to a nursing home but his kidneys started failing. I was with Mom in the emergency room on Christmas day because of her heart. My brother and I were going from the emergency room upstairs to be with my dad.

It is very surreal. We got Mom out of the hospital yesterday and took her home. She is supposed to get her heart shocked for the second time on January 3. This will depend on when Dad passes. I really do not want to lose him now. I do not want to lose another loved one this year. Mark, my sister-in-law in October, now Dad. God has a plan, I just know it.

My brother Danny, who lost his wife, has the flu. My other brother, Alan, had to take his wife to get her kidney stones broken up today. The grace in all of this is that my son, Robert, is getting leave from the Navy and will be here tomorrow. So he will get to see his Pop Pop, we hope, before he dies. That is our prayer. My mom is so sad and has her heart condition. They would have been married sixty-two years in February, 2013.

It has been quite the two weeks…here we go again. God's timing, not ours.

Rescue

"Grief wraps around people, takes them to a place they
would not go otherwise." —Patti Callahan

Well, bud, it was a year ago today that you went home. On one hand, it seems like a lifetime since I have seen you, talked to you and touched you. Sometimes it seems like another life. A year ago, something happened that changed my life. It was a nightmare that night…a nightmare. But for you, it was a joyful homecoming. For me it has been quite the year here without you. How I miss you!

Grief is a very lonely place. It is different for everyone and no one can understand but the one going through it. It is a path that you and you alone walk. But in my experience, Jesus entered this place with me…this journey. Jesus knows pain, loss and how to heal. No family member, no friend can understand but Jesus. It is a lonely journey through the valley of the shadow of death. But it is okay because even though you may feel alone you are not. And it is okay because Mark, I know you are now full of love and joy. That is my saving grace through all of this: you are at peace…you are home. But my home is not the same.

The memories of us as a family with Robert (what a great dad you were) and our times together are forever etched in my heart and mind. The good memories, the bad memories, the tears and the laughter. I have found that time eases the pain but it does not erase you from my heart. Mark—your smile, your touch, your laugh, your warm embrace and your love. Just you. I will always have a place in my heart for you, my surfing dude, Mark the Shark.

I am just telling you, honey, it has been a pain that I had not known before. A pain that I find hard to articulate and express with words. A pain that made me want to curl up in a corner and cry out, "God, take me...please. Just take me with him. I do not want to be here anymore. I do not want to live without you, Mark." A pain that made me physically sick. There were times I thought my heart could not find one more heartbeat because it was literally broken. It was shattered into tiny pieces. I wondered if it would ever be put back together again. What happened to my life? My family? My home? Our friends? There is such darkness in losing a loved one. It is then and only then that I believe any of us really looks at death, at life. I think it is in the death of someone we love that we make the decision to live or die. Do we die with them or do we live a new life without them? Do we lie down and quit or do we get stronger and persevere? Exactly what are we to do with the life we have left? Life we are all just a breath away from death and entering eternal life.

Bud, because of who you were, and of the hope I have in God, and because of what I learned being married to you. I learned that by losing you I made the decision to live without you, persevere and become stronger and better until I come home. Mark, we went through so much together. Our faith grew together. We were challenged through sickness, the loss of financial security, the loss of those we loved, the loss of our home. People took advantage of your trust and financial success leaving you with holding the debt that they owed you. And all you would say is, "Jesus may love you but I am having a hard time." We at times were the best of friends and then there were times we thought we were enemies. We were challenged in our marriage but we always worked it out. In the end, we grew closer because of the trials we faced. Dammit...I thought we would grow old together. I guess God had different plans.

I remember writing in my journal last New Year's Day like it was yesterday. I wrote about how we were going to have a great year. We were in this rented oceanfront condo...which you loved because you could give the wave report from the deck. I can still see you sitting in that chair, staring out at the ocean with your headphones on, listening to your favorite tunes, drinking your coffee…and finally at peace from all the struggles we encountered financially. I was journaling about how excited I was about the New Year because it was going to be like a honeymoon. It was just you and me since we got together. We had always had Robert because he was almost three at the time. We raised him together and were so proud that he had joined the Navy. It was only mutual that we were excited about our life together. You and me in this beach bungalow. The New Year looked promising. However, nine days later you were gone. Life had its own plans and we were not advised about it at all. Someone said to me after the death of their loved one that it felt like they had no control over anything anymore. We don't, do we? At least not over our circumstances. The only control we have is how we react to and handle those circumstances.

Mark, this year without you has been filled with so many emotions, challenges, highs and lows. There were times when I thought I could not stop the flood of tears that came and times when I could not shed a tear. I have made some very stupid decisions and some very wise decisions. I have felt pain so deeply that I did not want it to stop because it was better than feeling numb. I have been so lonely at night, only to wake up in the morning with a renewed spirit. I have been full of fear of the future, only to be challenged by that same fear to face it and do positive things within it. I have become so angry with God only to find that He loves me more than I ever knew. Even when I backed away, He never ever left me. He has always been by my side. He has carried me through every one of my dark, angry days. My faith has changed so much through this. It has humbled me and made me look at my walk with Jesus…what it was and what it is. I no longer see my walk with Him the way it was. I see people differently—I love them more. I see the world differently—I love life more. God is love. A love that I have never known.

I have seen friends who I never thought would leave me but I have also seen friends stand by me when I never thought they would. I have made new friends and renewed old friendships. It amazes me how easy it is to find out who your real friends are when something like this happens. And it is okay. It is good to know these things and I still love them all.

Mark, you would have been so proud of your cousin who was like a brother, Billy. He has walked with me through all of this. He helped me get out and move forward. He made me laugh. We have talked and cried together…about you…over you. And we have gotten mad at you for leaving us here. He misses you so much, as do I.

I could not have gotten through this year without my friends' love and support, our river days, my surfing days with my surfing buddies Inga and Sunyata. Oh, how I looked forward to surfing with those two beautiful girls. You would be so proud of me, Mark, for surfing even in cold water. The river, skiing, the healing of the ocean, working out, running, my personal training, my family at the gym, my coaching, taking continuing education courses, boxing, moving forward, growing, learning new things, playing, and working. It is the combination of all these things that have carried me through and helped me heal.

Mark, I remember us holding hands walking down the sidewalk and talking about a name for my business. I asked you to help me with a name…something feminine, but strong. And you said, "Name it Sweet Strength." You always believed more in me than I believed in myself…as I did with you, bud. I always believed more in you than you did. You always told me I was smart and beautiful and that I could do anything. You made me feel special. You were special. I miss your encouragement but I thank you for my name, Sweet Strength. Somehow it has given me the strength to encourage others and it has made me want to continue this journey, even without you. It has given me a purpose.

Thank you, Mark, for seventeen and half good—no—*great* years. The best years of my life. You may be gone but you will never be forgotten. You rock, my friend, and I will see you when I come home.

The Fall

"Man maintains his balance, poise, and sense of security only as he is moving forward" —*Maxwell Maltz*

For some time, I felt like I walked a balance beam of faith. Like I was walking that beam, that thin line, teeter-tottering between the different sides that lay beneath. If I lost my balance and fell to one side, it would crush me. I would become weak and helpless. I would lose my faith, my perseverance, my life, my peace, who I was and my purpose. I would fall flat on my face, never to recover because life was so hard and I was so very tired. I was tired of life, tired of losing those I love, of illness and of working to rebuild my life. Tired of my work due to not being in the workplace for so long because I was a mom and wife. Tired of seeing those I love in pain…tired of looking at hate, war, prejudice, hunger and death.

Then there was the other side of that fall, when I had land on my feet, ready to run, ready to face life instead of death, ready to encourage others because of what I had seen and been through, ready to live my life with meaning and purpose, ready to have peace instead of anxiety, ready to run the race marked out for me instead of giving in, ready to succeed, ready to grow stronger and stronger, ready to heal instead of hurt, ready to become the person that God had created me to be and ready to stand tall in victory Yes, ready for everything that life would throw at me because I would know that in my inner being I have a force. A power that compelled me forward, making me stronger than anything that would try to conquer me, calling me to live out my purpose to love others and have hope for better days. I believe I was made to stand, not fall; to love, not hate; to conquer, not quit; to inspire, not tear down; to give, not receive; to make peace, not war; to live life every moment of every day; to forgive as others have forgiven me; to reach for the stars; to dream; to take care of myself so I can take care of others; to be thankful for the illusion of time between sunrise and sunset; to hope for a better day.

I have felt for some time like I do not know which side I will fall toward. I especially had this very vivid view yesterday of walking that beam and thinking to myself that I could go either way after this. I really could. After losing three family members within a year, trying to build a business and losing everything financially. It has been not only a long year but a long five years. First there was my husband. Then in October, 2012, it was my sister in law. My brother's wife of thirty-four years. My niece and nephew's mom. I tell you it was a rough day for my family on that faithful day October 12, 2012 as any death in the family is. Making arrangements for my sister in law with my family brought back that day we did that with Mark, except I was not as numb. It is difficult to watch your brother go through the pain of losing his wife of thirty-four years unexpectedly. It is hard because you know the pain he will have to endure as the days turn into lonely nights and haunting memories of what used to be. It is hard to watch your niece and nephew lose their mom at such a young age. Donna was a wonderful woman. We had lots of fun and she would do anything for you. She loved her family so much. She had been in my life since I was sixteen and she was like a sister to me. We had so many good times together, shared life's secrets and helped each other through the child rearing ages. I miss her friendship and love. Donna always had the ability to make you laugh. Her and Mark were the jokesters in the family. They were so funny together. We spent a lot of time together sharing our lives, our losses, our children's experiences and so much more. I will miss her greatly.

Two months later, I watched my daddy die, lying on that bed, looking like a man I had never known, I was thinking I may teeter toward the side of despair and weakness. And then the following day watching my mom pick out his casket. Death and life, living and dying, dying to live, or living to die—or is there a line that separates the two? I mean, we must die to live. We must all face death to live or we will surely all die. My mom was so fragile, so sad, picking out how she wanted to see her husband of almost sixty-two years put in the ground. His external body which was not him really. But that is how we know and love our loved ones, is it not? We interact through our bodies, our touch, our voices, our faces and our smiles. Perhaps, we interact through the pain we share in our bodies, our tears. Yes, God's grace is to give us a face and a body to love and hug, to argue and make up with...to hold. God's grace gave us this way to feel a touch, to hear a voice and to see a smile. God's grace, it always amazes me.

As we made arrangements for my dad in the very room that we had been in two months earlier to make arrangements for my sister-in-law. I thought to myself, I am very close to falling over and landing on my face. It was almost as if I was not there. I was watching myself closely on that balance beam...walking...trying not to fall yet...trying to make the decision on which way to go. I remembered Mark and making those arrangements for him. I felt sorry for myself. All while knowing that others have losses too so which way am I going to fall? How do I stay balanced on this beam in the midst of this crazy, surreal scene in this funeral home? The funeral home director's voice was like that of the adults in the *Peanuts* cartoons...blah...blah...blah...blah...I looked at Mom, wondering if she was walking that same beam. She has had such a hard life. She was so strong but so weak. I thought how happy I was that Mark, Donna and Dad did not have to walk that beam anymore. The beam that leads us to Jesus brought each of them to a healed, loved, and at perfect peace.

I wonder sometimes why we have to walk that beam at all and why things cannot be easy. Why do we have to choose a side? I read something today in one of my favorite books and I was reminded that it is these times that make or break us is where we build up or tear down, make love or hate, make bitter or better that is why we always have that solid beam beneath us—Jesus. Because if we keep our feet on the beam and do not let distractions and circumstances get us off balance, we will not have to worry about which side we will fall. We will simply make the choice to jump off and land on our feet then take off running the race that is set before us.

"Contrary to what might be expected, I look back on experiences that at the time seemed especially desolating and painful with particular satisfaction. Indeed, I can say with complete truthfulness that everything I have learned in my seventy-five years in this world, everything that has truly enhanced and enlightened my existence, has been through affliction and not through happiness, whether pursued or attained. In other words, if it ever were to be possible to eliminate affliction from our earthly existence by means of some drug or other medical mumbo jumbo…the result would not be to make life delectable, but to make it too banal and trivial to be endurable. This, of course, is what the cross signifies, and it is the cross, more than anything else, that has called me inexorably to Christ." —Malcolm Muggeridge

For today, I am still balancing . . .because I hurt and I am not ready yet to fall on either side . . . just simply need to feel the beam beneath my feet.

The Married Life

"A great marriage is not when the "perfect couple comes together. It is when an imperfect couple learns to enjoy their difference."
— Dave Meurer

I miss the married life and most of all miss the one I was married to. It is hard to adjust some days but I am. I know there is good in the midst of all of this and that one day I will be on the other side. There is nothing on earth that can replace a great relationship full of fun, laughter and intimacy. There is nothing that can replace learning together with the one you love. There is nothing that can replace even the times of misunderstanding and arguments. It is in those times where you think there will be enough time in the day to make up and have the gentleness and freshness of making a compromise. Sometimes we forget that there is no point in getting stuck in the little stuff. Time is too short for arguing and not playing together and not loving one another.

Fake It Until You Make It

"Your biggest challenge isn't someone else, or your circumstance. It's the ache in your lungs, the burning in your legs, and the voice inside you that yells, 'Can't!' But you don't listen, you push harder. You hear the voice whisper 'Can,' and you discover that the person you thought you were is no match for the one you really are." —Unknown

It has been one year and a little over two months and it has been one of the most challenging experiences of my life. Losing Mark, my partner. I have been through a lot of difficult times and have experienced a lot in life. But the death of my husband trumps it all. Two thousand twelve was quite the year of deaths for my family. First Mark then my brother lost his wife of thirty-four years, my sister-in-law, Donna. Both Mark and Donna were in their early fifties. Then Dad on New Year's Eve. Mom lost her husband of sixty-one years.

I will never forget when Donna died. I was on the river on a warm day: October 12th, 2012. My oldest brother, Alan, called me and said they could not find my sister-in-law. She had gone to the cabin that Danny, my brother, had built and was not answering their calls. They lived by the beach but had a cabin on the farm where my family grew up. The door was locked, but her car was there. Her husband, Danny, was working and had asked my other brother, Alan, to check on her. Alan, said to me, "You may need to come home." As I headed in to get ready to help, I got the dreaded phone call. I call them the cold calls because they seem so cold…so distant…so foreign. Donna's body had been found inside of the cabin. She had suddenly died at fifty-four years old.

Danny and my sister-in-law had been together for thirty-four years. Thirty-four years! I had grown up with Donna; it seemed she had always been in my life. She and Mark loved to cut up and joke. Now they were together.

I remember my brother Danny saying to me, "I will be fine; I will get through this easier than you." I said, "No, you won't. No, you won't." It was the shock. He was trying to absorb the shock of someone alive and present yesterday and gone today. There is no smooth way to experience that transition. There is no easy way.

I remember being at the funeral home, thinking, here we go again with arrangements. I felt nauseated. It was too soon to be there again. Too soon to feel those emotions rushing through again. I was just beginning to feel steady again. But life is not steady. Life is a never-ending journey of change that wants to test our balance. It took every fiber of strength I had to try and be there for my brother and my parents.

Mom and Dad seemed to float in and out of the hospital that year. They were not able to come to any of the funerals. Mom hated it and felt so guilty. She wanted to help me but was doing all she could to take care of herself and Dad. She is a strong woman—a woman who knows firsthand about "Sweet Strength." She grew up during the Depression, with a mom who had depression. Mom and I talked daily and encouraged each other.

Then that December, the week before Christmas, my oldest brother called me. Mom had fallen and Dad wasn't doing well—bronchitis, they thought. So the doctor was admitting both of my parents to the hospital. In her fall, Mom had hit her head. She was fine, but needed to be under observation, and she was worn out. Dad had bronchitis and a progressive lung disease called Chronic Obstructive Pulmonary Disease (COPD).

The next thing we knew, dad's kidneys started failing. He had never had kidney issues before. On New Year's Day, our daddy—my mom's husband of sixty-one years—passed away. Another funeral, another set of arrangements to be made. Could we all do it again? What choice were we given? Death never gives us a choice.

Life and only life gives us the choice to live or die...we have to decide.

I do not remember much about my father's funeral or making the arrangements. I did realize that I could not grieve for Donna or Daddy because I had not even finished grieving for Mark.

Death and losing loved ones happens every day. It happens somewhere and to someone.

If I had known or someone had told me how hard it would be to continue to live each day to its fullest and not fall prey to the battle within my mind, I would have never believed them.

Beginning the very day after Mark went home, I realized if I did not choose to change everything about what I understood those seventeen years of my life and make it into something completely new. I would lose the battle between life and living...really living...and I would die.

I had been in this familiar, yet unfamiliar on a totally different level before with my thoughts and my mind. The games my mind will play on me at times. The war...the battle...the confrontation between thinking positively, creatively, optimistically and hopefully compared to thinking negatively, fearfully, confusedly, closed-mindedly and narrowly. The mental challenge to overcome circumstances that seem impossible to overcome. Circumstances that only myself, spirit and soul understand. Only the faith I have in God to get me through will lend a hand to the battle for my mind. My trust and faith have come from my Jesus.

We live in such a world that the media seem to thrive on turning diversity into negativity and focuses on every evil that happens. The media feeds this to us on a regular basis, regurgitating the same crap over and over again and we eagerly receive it like a mother bird's babies receive food. It is as if we do not have enough on our plates with everyday living. You hardly ever hear about the good things that are going on in the world, the hope and the miracles that occur every single day. You really have to make a conscious effort to change your mindset and perspective to look for the good and not the bad. You have to aspire to hear the positive in each situation, not the negative. It takes effort, especially in the fast-paced, high-tech, stressful environment in the society we live.

There have been many times during this completely new way of living that every fiber in me has told me to quit. My mind plays games with me. Especially when I am missing Mark, my family and my sense of security. I know my sense of security can be illusive at times because personally, my only security is Jesus.

There were days when I thought, what are you going to do? How are you going to live without Mark? How are you going to earn an income? Where are you going to live? You are not strong enough to do this, simply lie down and quit. Run and do not look back. Linda, you cannot do this alone.

My mind was tired, my heart was broken and I was confused and struggling in a different way with my faith. I felt alone (in the midst of so many people, I still felt very alone), and my body was exhausted. There were days when I did not want to get out of bed. There were days I did not feel like smiling, talking, or seeing anyone.

However, deep within my spirit and my soul, there is this small voice pushing me forward, enticing me to live differently. The same voice is challenging me to think differently, to be stronger, to be better, to not give up, to run with the horses and not walk with the turtles. Well...it was better than the other option. So each day, I made a choice...I made an effort…I made myself smile, get up, be positive, share my gifts and talents with those around me, work out, eat healthy, learn something new, be with friends, go out and just *move*. In other words, I knew that I needed to fake it until I could really make it. If you can think negatively then you can think positively. If you look for the bad then you will certainly find it if you look for the good and challenge your thoughts then you will find the best.

Our minds are a powerful gift we were given by our Creator. Our thoughts are what make our lives. They can either propel us to create a new us, hold us back or take us back to places we are not supposed to be. Thoughts involve the battles in our minds, and the challenges we face to stay motivated. Our minds need to be both positive and hopeful so that we have a purpose and an opportunity to share with others in life.

There were days when I literally talked out loud, arguing with myself about my thoughts and how I could be positive just as easily as I could be negative. How only I could make my life? How I could choose how my life is going to be lived out? I argued until the right voice was in the forefront of my thoughts: You are beautiful, you are talented, you love others, you have lots of support from family and friends and you have so much to offer. Your body, your health and your mind are given to you for a purpose.

That is how we relate to others—through our body and our words. They both need to be at their best for us to be able to care for or love others. We can bring sunshine to our lives and to the lives of others or we can bring hell to our lives and others'. It all begins with our thoughts. Everything in our world started with a thought…either a great thought or a bad one.

There are four questions by Byron Katie that have helped me when my thoughts want to run on the path to disaster. These questions come from a process she calls "The Work." It involves four questions that each believe may be the cause of pain: Is it true? Can you absolutely know that it's true?

How do you react when you believe that thought? Who would you be without the thought?

Sitting With Pain

"I can bear any pain as long as it has meaning." —Haruki Murakami

The dictionary describes pain as suffering, distress of body or mind. I feel so much pain right now…not that I have not before. Not that any of us have never felt pain. We have all carried the burden of pain in one way or another. Losing Mark has brought me much affliction in both my body and mind. Today, I cried out and said, "Lord have mercy on me. Please enter this place with me." I have embraced the realization that I have to learn to sit with this grief at times and let it come. That is the hard part: sitting and allowing Jesus to enter this place with me. I really want to numb it on days like this. Days when it gets so bad that I can only cry out for Jesus to have mercy on me. Those are about all the words I have today.

People want to cure my pain. People who love me want to take away my grief and how thankful I am for the people who love me and who loved Mark. Only God can enter my pain and sometimes in a strange and foreign way it is comforting to sit with my pain. It is comforting to not react to it and just sit with it, processing it. It provides great insight into who I am as a person. I know this is why God allows us to feel pain so that we may know Him more and to love others at greater depths. Those depths allow us to take a glimpse into our souls. I cannot even imagine the pain Jesus felt on that cross or the pain that God felt when He allowed Jesus, His one and only son, to be on that cross. Who could wrap their finite mind around something so far from our comprehension? Not me. I try but I cannot. Jesus, He sat in his pain and cried out in his pain. It is through His abundant grace He loved through the depth of pain.

One time when Robert, my son, was little there was a bad thunderstorm on the horizon. Lightning was crackling all around us and the thunder sounded like it was going to rattle every last pane of glass. Robert must have been about six or seven. I was upstairs reading a book to him, which was my favorite thing to do. He looked up at me and said, "Mom, I'm scared." Trying to be an optimistic mom, I said, "Robert, there is nothing to be scared of...all that lightning and thunder is how much power God has, and with that very power He watches over you. You do not have anything to be scared of. In fact, even if we were to die tonight in this storm, we would be alive with Jesus with all that power and glory." Robert looked up at me and said, "Mom, you always try to be positive...I just want to be scared for now; can I be scared?"

Today I simply wanted to feel my anguish to feel the loss which was okay to feel pain and not try to bury it or numb it and it was okay to sit with the pain, ponder it, get to know Jesus more intimately and get to know myself a little better. The bittersweetness that comes with the pain.

Pain can be covered up. Going through this grief I do it now and then and in the past have done it in unhealthy ways. Anything to stop the pain, the affliction. We do that, do we not? Immerse and enmesh ourselves with friends, exercise, music, wine, drugs, pornography, shopping, overeating, under-eating, overworking—you name it, we do it...anything to stop the pain. And we do not even recognize that it only prolongs and increases the pain. It is an illusion that it will help. There is only one thing to do which is to sit with it and let God enter it with you. It will pass. All emotions do. They are like visitors coming and going. Some visitors stay longer than others while some can be more intense. Then there are those that are more gentle, but eventually they all leave. If I sit with the sorrow, it passes more quickly than when I try to dull it with other distractions.

If we did not have pain then we would not be able to even begin to understand or appreciate the sweetness of life. We would not be able to empathize with others' pain nor would we ever see ourselves in a way that stops us. A way that slows us down, beckons us and calls us to transformation into the likeness of He who enters the pain with us. Jesus who knew real pain. He is the only one I know who dared to die for our pain, for our healing and for our life. We find out more regarding who God is, who we are and about who others are by sitting in silence in the unwelcome but necessary pain.

Not Stopping

Ever since Mark died I have felt like stopping.

Sometimes, I lie in bed at night wondering what happened to seventeen years of my life. I wonder how I got here especially when going home to an empty house night after night. I stare at the ceiling all while avoiding the trap of fear of the future. I eventually make myself regain control of my thoughts and bring them to the present where everything is good.

What a journey. I mean, it is an adjustment to go from partnership to figuring it all out on your own. Going from not having to worry about an income to learning to make one all while trying to build a successful business. We all have a journey to live out. We have to live it out and not stop because life does not stop for us. Life keeps on even if we decide to hang up the towel and attempt to stop life. It is only your life that will stop. Remember it is never over. It is not over until we stop.

Therefore, stopping is not an option. We have to keep moving. It is when we continue to move and to live life no matter the circumstances that we can then take responsibility for our lives. Even if the circumstances are beyond our control. It is imperative that responsibility is taken for our lives and for the choices we make. Our choice not to quit is by far the most important. If we stop then there is no option to improve. If we stop there is no opportunity to succeed. If we stop we will never reach our goals and our dreams will never have a chance. If we stop we may never have an opportunity to love again. If we stop we will never know what could have been.

We are here for a purpose: to live up to our full potential. That is what God has planned for us. He has a perfect plan for us but we cannot stop. We have to believe…we have to hope…and we have to see beyond what is in front of us.

In reality, my struggle does not matter. I can do this. I just have to say to myself, "Do not stop." It is always darkest before dawn. You are always about to break a barrier when you seem at your worst. You are always on the brink of success when you feel like you have failed. We cannot stop…because life does not stop for us.

Surfer Dude

"Sometimes, only one person is missing,
and the whole world seems depopulated"
—*Alphonse de Lamortino*

It is a beautiful day in the neighborhood. That is what Mark would say. This morning, a year and half later, I am thinking about my surfing dude. I guess the Surf Rider Expo this afternoon makes me think of his love and passion for surfing. It is not just surfing but the surf community and his large array of friends. He loved people and loved me so much.

I love this time of year. Spring and summer in the air—my favorite time. Mark and I would head to the beach; I loved watching him surf. He left such an impact on my life and on his friends' lives.

I hope on this day for those who knew Mark will remember his smile, his laughter, his love of the ocean, his love of surfing, his love of Jesus and his love of his friends. I hope they will remember the way he spread love. It was through being a best buddy one of the many gifts he had of making everyone feel special. I hope it will inspire them to do their best surfing and to be thankful that they live at the beach where they can surf (even though they may get frustrated because there may not be the waves they like). Mark always said, "If you can surf here, you can surf anywhere," and he proved it! I hope that knowing him inspires his friends to love others as they are, not as another person thinks they should be. I hope they never forget him but remember he would want them to live their lives to the fullest. He would want them to enjoy the moment, never in a hurry, enjoy who they are with, enjoy life, this ocean, this beach community and people.

Finding The Peace

"Peace is a journey of a thousand miles and it must be taken one step at the time." —Lyndon B. Johnson

This morning is cloudy…overcast, yet again…ugh…where is my morning sunrise, which compels me to get up and get going? Well…it failed this morning. It fell into a foggy, dreary day.

I typically get so excited in the morning. I love the thought of going on the beach and watching the sunrise and running. It just gives me hope that everything is going to be okay. It assures me that God has given me another day to spread sunshine to others. I just do not do well with the clouds and cold.

This morning, I decided I needed a bigger challenge than running my usual run on the beach. There are days I just need to push myself a little harder…to see if I can do it. Most days, I find the hard sand to run on. Because I was feeling a little down this morning, I knew that I needed that extra push so I decided to do my time on the soft sand.

Halfway through my time, I said to myself (yes, I talk to myself), "I can't do this. . . well, why can't you do it? Does your body say you can't? No. Do you not want to do it? Yes, I want to do it. Do you need to do it? That could be debated. Does your mind tell you to stop? Yes—that's it. It's my mind, not my body, that wants to stop. Well, Linda," I said to myself, "You have a choice, you know. There is no one out here. You are racing against no one but yourself. You can stop anytime…or you can do your time." That was what I needed to hear. "I can do this," I said. "I want to do this…I need to do this for myself." I run in soft sand once in a while, but this morning it seemed extremely difficult. I felt as if I were in quicksand at points. I felt as if I could not make my running stride…that I was bogged down—and I was. But I kept going until I met my time, so another challenge met…another struggle defeated. I had the patience, the fortitude and the peace that came with the accomplishment.

I thought, that is how I feel about my grieving process. I do not want to do the time. I am tired of the struggle. I do not want to continue going through this. And the grief is not just about losing Mark but it is also about losing who I was. It is about all the changes that have occurred since Mark's death. I usually thrive on a good challenge—I do not like it when I think I cannot do something or someone else says I cannot do something. It makes me work harder to accomplish it. But I do not have a lot of patience for this grieving process…so there are many times I have no peace. I believe peace and patience have to go together…like a pair of scissors that cannot cut unless both blades are there. Now, I know where my peace lies and to a certain extent I have that underlying peace propelling me to live the next day out. However, there are times I cannot find it. Times when I do not accept Jesus's gift of peace. I would rather struggle a little more.

A friend who is very special to me said, "Linda, you have to find peace in the midst of this process." I think she was really saying that I needed to be patient because if I have patience then I will have peace. To be patient with myself and with all the things I am dealing with financially. Mark usually made the financial decision that I now have to make. I am not used to this single life. I must have patience with others because the ones you think will be there so often are not and the ones you did not think would be there are.

I have to do my time in the grief process. I have to find the peace and the patience because I learned that whether I have the patience for this grief or not, it has the patience for me.

"Now, may the Lord of peace himself give you peace at all times in every way. The Lord be with you all" — *2 Thessalonians. 3:16.*

Move Just Move

"It takes courage to push yourself to places that you have never been before...to test your limits...to break through barriers. And the day came when the risk it took to remain tight inside the bud was more painful than the risk it took to blossom." —Anaïs Nin

This is certainly true in my life. This is what I experience as I walk through this season of grief. This time of reflection, of life—of living, not dying. There are so many things I do not want to do right now. But I find as time goes on that I am embracing life in a different way and that it would be so much more painful to stay here, in this place. I want to grow and learn through this time of change, this time of leaving the security of the known to move into uncertainty. I want to experience life in a new way. I want to be the woman that God created me to be

I want to take risks to love, to grow, to give, to be stretched, to run, and not walk, to soar like an eagle and to live life to the fullest while taking care of myself so I can be of value to others.

I do not weep for Mark. Mark is good—he is better than good. He is at his best and being loved more than our humanity can even comprehend. Instead, I get sad when I do not move forward, when I feel frozen. I weep for those who cannot move past pain and grief and are immobilized. I weep for those who cannot break through the barriers. I know because I have experienced, not only in this, but during other painful times in my life. It is so much better to blossom through risking it all than to remain inside the bud.

We are here just for a short time; we are not promised tomorrow. It is critical to live in awareness of the life going on around us and in us. And to do those things we have always dreamed about doing so we can become the people God created us to be.

Run With The Horses

I have a painting of horses running hanging above my computer. I love it because it reminds me of one of my favorite verses in scripture. "If you have raced with men on foot and they have wearied you, how will you compete with the horses? And if in a safe land you fall down, how will you do in the jungle of the Jordan?" —Jer. 12:5

Eugene Peterson wrote a book about Jeremiah called *Run with the Horses*. In it, he talks about this verse:

> There is a memorable passage concerning Jeremiah's life when, worn down by the opposition and absorbed in self-pity, he was about to capitulate to such a premature death. He was ready to abandon his unique calling in God and settle for being a Jerusalem statistic. At that critical moment he heard the reprimand. Biochemist Erwin Chargaff updates the questions: "What do you want to achieve? Greater riches? Cheaper chicken? A happier life, a longer life? Is it power over your neighbors that you are after? Are you only running away from your death? Or are you seeking greater wisdom, deeper piety?"
>
> Life is difficult, Jeremiah. Are you going to quit at the first wave of opposition? Are you going to retreat when you find that there is more to life than finding three meals a day and a dry place to sleep at night?…Are you going to live cautiously or courageously? I called you to live at your best, to pursue righteousness, to sustain a drive toward excellence. It is easier, I know, to be neurotic. It is easier to be parasitic. It is easier to relax in the embracing arms of The Average. Easier, but not better. Easier, but not more significant. Easier, but not more fulfilling. I called you to a life of purpose far beyond what you think yourself capable of living and promised adequate strength to fulfill your destiny. Now at the first sign of difficult you are ready to quit? What is it you really want, Jeremiah? Do you want to shuffle along with the crowd, or run with the horses?[5]

I want to run with the horses. Mark would want me to do that, too.

---

[5] Eugene H. Peterson, *Run with the Horses (Downers Grove, IL: IVP Books, 2010).*

The Raspberry

I love this short story that is inscribed on five of the six pillars in the Holocaust Memorial in Boston's Quincy Market. The stories speak of the cruelty and suffering that was endured in the camps. The story I love follows:

> The sixth pillar presents a tale of a different sort, about a little girl named Ilse, a childhood friend of Guerda Weissamn Kline, in Auschwitz. Guerda remembers that Ilse, who was about six years old at the time, found one morning a single raspberry somewhere in the camp. Ilse carried it all day long in a protected place in her pocket, and in the evening, her eyes shining with happiness, she presented it to her friend Guerda on a leaf. "Imagine a world," writes Guerda, "in which your entire possession is one raspberry, and you give it to your friend."

I would give my raspberry to Mark, my best friend. In fact, I would give all my possessions to have him back one more time…just to see him once more, to hear him, to feel him. But one day soon I will be able to give him my raspberry, as we will be together with hope and love for eternity. Can you imagine the eyes in which Ilse looked through? The soul…what she experienced: the pain she felt, the fear? It was real, not imagined. And yet through this pain and fear she chose to see the sweetness of one raspberry and the love that drives out all fear…and she extended that love, that one sweet glance of life in the middle of death. She let love rule. It was probably the only piece of food she had in a long time…probably the only piece of life she had witnessed in a long time…probably the only piece of color in that godforsaken place that she had seen…and she chose to give that precious gift to her friend. In the midst of suffering, of fear, of control and of death she chose friendship and love. She chose to live.

I doubt anyone I know or most of us have ever experienced what Guerda and Ilse did in their little six-year-old lives but some have. Some people have experienced so much horrific pain that I wonder how they survived to tell their story. Pain, depression, suffering—it is all relative to what we know. Relative to what we have grown up with and experienced as individuals, as Americans and as free people. Pain is so different for everyone. It really does not matter what someone else may think pain is or how hard it is to endure. We all have it, precious pain. We all cling to a certain fear. We all hide some kind of scars, sins and guilt. It all gives us a reason to give up. We can find all kinds of excuses because of it and abandon our goals and our plans. Hell, it can cause us to abandon our lives, our hope, our reason for pressing on to love and give to others. It can cause us to give up those dreams that lie dormant at the bottom of our shattered hearts and souls. Pain can give us a reason not to change. It keeps us in invisible chains but Ilse saw life in the pain. She saw love in giving the only thing she had to offer: that raspberry. Maybe, just maybe love would be enough to free her and her friend from the dark walls that surrounded them. Maybe love would drive out their fear.

I ran into a friend of mine in the grocery store today and she was in pain. She was depressed. She said she had been that way for two years and that she could not feel God. I talked with her for a short while and had much empathy for her pain. She said she felt so alone. Oh, how I could relate. Yes, I think we can all relate at one time or another to loneliness. But without loneliness we would not be able to understand what it is to not be alone. We would not be able to understand love.

I have felt so displaced since Mark died. Felt kind of lost. But if I was not lost, I would not know what home was. Home is found in your heart, a cliché, but so true.

You know, loneliness is designed to help you discover who you are and to help you stop looking outside yourself for your worth. I bet that on that day, Ilse knew who she was. She did not look outside of herself. She discovered love, a love so sweet, a love of who she was so she could think of nothing else but giving.

I tried to understand my friend who has been struggling with depression. I tried to have empathy for her pain and loneliness as I could definitely relate to her not feeling God. I know that as I give to others, as I try to inspire and encourage others and try to move in my pain, I feel God there. I feel joy, not pain. I feel hope because you have to give that last possession to live, to love and to feel. I pray that my friend will pick the raspberry, put it in her pocket and give it to another so she will lose her chains of pain…of fear…of loneliness.

I wonder if Ilse "felt God" in that godforsaken place. I told my friend that if she waited to feel God again, it may never come. You have to know He is there. To be honest with you, I rarely "feel" God but I know He is there. He is in my soul. He created me and I trust He is there. Otherwise, I would have never made it this far and I sure as hell would not have gotten out of bed after Mark died.

I bet Ilse knew that God was with her. How else could she give her last possession to her friend? How else could she have *joy* in the midst of darkness? How else could God have given His last possession for us to live—Jesus? God gave him to us, his friends. We did not earn it. There is nothing we can do to earn it and nothing we can say to be given pure love. God did not base it on a feeling. It was based on something bigger than a feeling. It was based on an action of love.

Love, you might be surprised to know is not a feeling it is an action. It is willing good to another person. The feelings come as fruit to love. Ilse performed the action of love. I hope that we would all have the possibility in our hearts to be like Ilse.

Somehow, I know that if we could reach that state of giving our last possession for love all our fears would be driven out.

Come Sit Down

"If you have no time for rest, it's exactly the right time."
— *Mark Twain*

As I begin my rest and respite for the week, a much needed break…I realize I have not had a break mentally, emotionally or physically since my husband died. I am tired. We all need breaks. I am so wired and Mark used to be the one to say, "Linda, come sit down with me. Come sit and relax. Linda, let's enjoy where we are, not where we are going next." He was the most laid-back guy and I was full of energy. We were different in so many ways but it was a yin-and-yang kind of relationship. I knew how to keep the excitement and he knew how to calm me down and ground me. One night I was painting as I had been all day. Mark sat on the couch and was watching me paint. I said, "You could help." And he said, "Or you could sit down on the couch beside me and relax, It will be here tomorrow." He knew how to calm me.

Oh, I miss that in my life. The yin to my yang. I have not had that other side of balance in my life since he died. I am having to learn to be the yin and yang in myself. I am learning to be whole without Mark. That in itself is a journey and a learning process. He was my calmness in the midst of my overzealous passion to move and go and do and my desire to empower others to live with zest, passion, health, and self-love.

I of course can coach others in peace, calmness and stress management. Is that not the way it usually works? I mean, I am trained in it. It is very hard for me. I have been working on it. In due time I am getting there. I take time. Often it is in the activeness of my life that I find peace and renewal. I gain inner strength through building my business and engaging in activities such as water skiing, boxing, weight training, surfing and other things that keep me active. Being active is my peace and my healing. However, I need complete rest now. I will have no schedule for a week, no expectations and no agenda. I will live in the present, in nature and with those I love. I will not coach, train, or engage in business-building. I will allow myself to just be, rest and listen to God. God, the one who calls me to rest.

Angels Come in Many Forms

"Angels appear in many different forms to hold your hand through difficult times." —Doreen Virtue

I decided to walk on the beach earlier. Sometimes I just need to slow down. I have been running as fast as a cheetah runs after its prey since Mark died. I still have not caught my prey. I am still running. You see, Mark was gone a second after he died. My belief is I have to move forward even a second ago is the past. Besides, if I slow down, the past that is gone pounces on me and traps me. The loneliness wants to hold me hostage but I do not dare stay there because it threatens to keep me prisoner allowing no hostage bargaining or release.

As I walked, my angel hostage negotiator showed up in the form of a seagull. He followed me down the beach as if to talk with me. During Mark's paddle-out there was a lone seagull that flew over us. I know it was that same seagull walking with me today. It let me share my pain so I would not be captured by it, but instead released from it. That seagull followed me all the way to my path back home and he flew away when the tears were gone. God sent an angel to carry the weight of the pain away.

73

Free Bird

Would you still remember me?
For I must be traveling on now
'Cause there's too many places I've got to see.
But if I stayed here with you, girl, Things just couldn't be the same.

'Cause I'm as free as a bird now,
And this bird you cannot change, oh, oh, oh, oh.
And this bird you cannot change.

This is for us, Mark. It has been a year and half later and we are both free on different sides of the world. I look forward to the day when all is completed with my side of the world and we are all free to be with you and God. Free to believe and accept his gracious offering of everlasting life. "Free Bird" reminds me of Mark and our journey to our separate worlds.

I often think of stories I have read of people who die and are hovering over their bodies. They are looking down at loved ones, at the nurses and doctors who are trying to save them. They are then presented with a question or a conversation allowing them to go with the light or stay with their families. They are given a glimpse of the other side. A side of indescribable beauty and everlasting life with unconditional love shared with those who have gone before them.

Of course you only hear the stories of those who return to life.

I often think of Mark doing this exact scenario, one where he is watching me frantically try to bring him back to life but debating if he should stay or go. Mark had lots of family whom he loved and passed before him. He told me several times that he was ready to go. He had a lot of stress here on earth. I know he loved me and wanted to stay with me but the pull of freedom and unconditional love held him that afternoon. It comforted him. It was his time and the decision was made. He was going home. Home to be totally free once and for all.

I picture him making that hard decision but the only one he could. We all need to be free. We need to be free from worry and stress, free to love, free to give and free to accept the grace and forgiveness that Jesus has so freely offered us. Some of us learn how to be free on this side of the world. I believe when you can learn to be free with yourself, who you are and who God created you to be, you become a free bird. You begin to have a small taste of the freedom that is offered in another world. A world that offers pure unconditional love and grace. Our true home will be when we enter the gates of heaven…our true home. All you have to do is believe.

Mark your freedom is true freedom. I remain humble and thankful for the freedom I have left here on earth. I am free to love my singleness, to love others, to love myself and to accept and believe what is offered by our Savior. Our Savior offers everlasting love, unconditional love and a home with no pain and no suffering. Love, until it is my time we shall be free in two different worlds.

Invisible Walls

"Limitations tend to be illusions or self-created barriers."
—*Steven Redhead*

When I run on the beach in the mornings there is a place I cannot seem to pass. Since the death of Mark I have not been able to run past the condos that Mark built. I always turn around when I reach them. There are too many memories and too many reminders of unanswered prayers. It is funny how we have these walls in front of us that seem so silly but they are so real in our heads.

The condos Mark built in 2007 became the beginning of the end for both Mark and I financially, emotionally, and physically. At the time there was no risk in building condos. However, the real estate market at that time was unstable. Six million people lost their homes and financial security.

For years I would run to those condos and pray over them. I would pray that they would sell and Mark would keep his health. Then Mark had his heart attack, and he thought surely they would sell. Of course, they didn't. We even had people come and pray with us. I tried to get Mark to let them go into foreclosure but he could not bring himself to do so, he was always a man. He said he had to do what he could to keep going and making payments. The banks wouldn't work with him at all. He tried everything he could. Ultimately, we lost everything. The condos, our home and our financial security. We had the best home. It was built in 1935 by a New York Architect. Mark loved older homes. He researched and found out who the owners and the architect were. There was no landscaping when we bought the house so we got the advantage of creating what we wanted. Mark loved this. He designed the pool and worked with the landscaper on the design of the yard, plants and trees we wanted. I loved palm trees. We planted nine around our pool. The big joke with our landscaper was "More Palm Trees Please" because I loved them so much. There was this stream in the backyard and beyond the stream was an area of wild growth and bamboo. Mark loved going back there to work and cut back the overgrowth with his big machete. That is how he relieved his stress. We always knew where to find Mark if he had a stressful day. He was either in the water surfing or cutting down extra bamboo. He was so proud of that house and it was so unique. We lived there over thirteen years before we lost it to foreclosure. He was devastated.

He never truly healed from all the loss.

God never answered my prayers at least not in the way I wanted them answered. The condos did not sell and we lost our home. Ultimately God did not answer my prayers of keeping Mark healthy either.

Mark, you are free from that now. You do not owe money to anyone. You do not owe one penny. You carry no debt now. Honey, it is all okay now.

I have had this huge wall in front of me when at those condos. I have tried to go around that wall (run past those condos in the mornings) and it just seems to stretch so far that I can never find the end. . . So I turn back. I have tried scaling that wall only to find myself sliding back down and landing on my back. The weight of my body making an imprint in the sand...only to get up, turn around and go back. Maybe I changed and I thought that could pole vault over that wall. In the end I always came up short and the wall just seemed too high.

This morning I decided I was just going to surrender to that wall and that I needed to pray. I should possibly thank Him for this wall, this barrier and give it to Him to handle. I closed my eyes, stretched out my arms and I ran right through that wall. I ran right through the center of that concrete wall. I ran right past those condos. I kept running and crying and then running. Guess what I discovered? It did not stop me that it was not hard at all. There was no wall, only a mere illusion. I imagined it and had built it there.

What a great feeling being from barriers I now had freedom from the walls we built and stopped us from praying, to be from hoping and from moving forward. False illusions only appear to be real. I did it Mark!

Traveling Abroad

As we head into fall and into twenty-one months later, it is bittersweet for me. One, because summer is coming to a close and it's my favorite time of the year. The hotter, the better for me…maybe it is because I was born in June. I am a flip-flop, bathing-suit, water-fun kind of girl. Another reason is that it means memories of loss come creeping in.

This summer has been tougher for me than last summer. July through September has been quite the battle for me, emotionally. It seems the longer my husband has been gone, the quieter it gets, and the stillness is just plain spooky at times. I am a people person and love being in a relationship and this experience has really given me another perspective on those who have lost loved ones, relationships and live alone. It has given me empathy for those who feel like they're walking alone in this world, even if they are surrounded by friends. Empathy for those in a foreign land.

Those of us who feel as if we are traveling alone in a foreign land for the first time surrounded by multitudes of people but no one seems to speak our language. We feel totally displaced as we try to learn fragments of the language. We can ask for directions to fit in and we can navigate around their streets and community. No one wants to feel like they are displaced or lost.

Yes, the attack from that enemy called loneliness snuck up on me like a cat sneaks up—slowly but with perfect pouncing precision on her prey. The single little sparrow busy finding straw for her new nest does not even notice what lurks behind her.

What an emotional battle it has been. I am thankful I have my protective shield around me. Without God it would have been tough to get through these last months unscathed from the soreness caused by loneliness's laceration.

My battle with loss and loneliness is that: a battle. It is not the end, it is the beginning. The beginning of finding my adventure in a new land. It brings opportunities for new relationships, new sights and a new way of living. It is kind of like after you get rid of the anxiety and fear of being in that foreign land alone. You start to want to thrive there. You want to enjoy it. You begin to learn and understand the language of those around you better. You begin to learn about the area...you get a road map...you ask for directions...you suddenly find the streets in the community becoming more familiar. You are finding your way around. You are beginning to feel more comfortable in your own skin, even though you may feel a little different on the inside. You are starting to understand the culture. You are even starting to dress like the natives. The foreign land becomes another part of who you are. . .

When you know it is time to go home to what you know, the familiar. You will have gained from your experiences in that foreign land. You will have become stronger. You will be able to understand those around you better. You will be able to help them navigate through a foreign land because you learned how to do so. You will look at those you love differently because you will be empathetic, remembering that they may be in a foreign land too...learning their way around.

The Line Up

"Her happiness floated like waves of ocean along the coast of her life. She found lyrics of her life in his arms but she never sung her song."
—*Santosh Kalwar*

Some mornings, I love to walk down to where the surfers are and watch them in the lineup. The sight is absolutely beautiful; it is so serene watching all of them waiting for their opportunity to do what they love best. Riding the wave as it rolls in against the beautiful vast horizon of the deep blue sea as the sun prepares for its day to rise high in the September sky. They make surfing look so easy but that is the talent of any good athlete. When they are engaged in their favorite sport they make it look as easy as walking.

I like to look for Mark in the lineup. It brings me peace, thinking I may see him or at least envision him out there. I keep thinking if I look hard and long enough, maybe I will see a glimpse of his white hair and his style of controlling his board; moving it where he wants it to go on the wave…carving out his own style with each drop-in…making his presence known without having to say, "Here I am, look at me! Look at me master this wave!" He loved surfing…the water…his friends. And he was humble. I loved that about him.

I often asked him why he did not try to make surfing his career. He would tell me that his mom got sick and he felt he needed to help his dad with the motel and get his college degree. It was like Mark, sacrificing for others. That is who he was. He never lost his love of surfing and the salt water, which kept drawing him back, wave after wave.

Yes, I know I would not really see him in the water when I look for him. It is just a place to connect my mind, heart, spirit and soul because sometimes your mind and heart want to tell you something different. They are not in sync with each other. So I have to learn how to get them on the same page. After all, we are all one heart, mind, body, spirit and soul. To heal and be whole, I have to solve the mystery of keeping the inside and outside on the same wavelength.

I may never be a great surfer, but it is a place that brings me peace because I feel Mark's spirit...because I'm sitting in the middle of God's creation, which is so much bigger than me. It humbles me. It brings me peace because I'm surrounded by others who are there for their own reasons and their own passion for surfing. It heals me. It congeals my heart, body, soul, and spirit together in a rhythm. The ocean...the peace...the action...learning a new skill moves me forward. It keeps me strong and moving forward in life, which I have done since Mark died. I have moved forward, not staying in the grief...not staying in the sadness of it all.

I searched for the place where I could feel peace that transcends all understanding. I needed a real place to pull it all back together when it wants to come unraveled. I also understand that for me it was someone bigger than myself who pointed me to that place. Jesus Christ continues to give me strength. Without Him, I would not have the inner strength to enjoy this life that I do not always understand. He gives me a survival instinct that will not let me give in. He gives me hope that this is not all there is but that this is what I have now. I need to live it to the fullest: laugh, give to others and above all have fun!

A day does not go by that I do not think of Mark and miss him. I know he would want me to continue my life, because he would be the first to let me know that life is short.

SWEET STRENGTH IS ALWAYS MOVING FORWARD WITH A ZEST FOR LIFE.

Familiar Brown Chair

"We are torn between nostalgia for the familiar and an urge for the foreign and strange. As often as not, we are homesick most for the places we have never known." — Carson McCullers

They come so suddenly as I slide into my favorite chair with a journal and pen and a cup of hot green tea comfortably held in my hands. I was really hoping that the time had come…that the drops would not come. I mean, it has been a while since I sat here. I mean it is close to two years. Surely, I thought, they will not come this time.

Avoidance is so comforting when you do not want to be in a familiar place…a spot that takes your memories on an emotional ride to another place and time. It gets tiring sometimes having to face reality and then battle. The battle always brings freedom with it. Reality is like an internal dialogue. It has a blatant voice that I would just as soon not hear…especially today…because this morning, I was dancing with a stranger called a new life until I melted into this chair of familiarity.

By all accounts, I am doing great with this new change and I love who I am becoming. However today, there is no avoiding who I was. One by one…pain by pain…the moisture falls so effortlessly, containing who I was and holding the joy of who I am becoming. The tears roll down my cheek falling on my freshly composed thoughts while smearing and staining my paper. Dammit. I hate this. I hate being weak and afraid. I do not like falling victim to my own cocooning memories of who I was, my life before or to the fearful thoughts that threaten to hamper the release of this new, beautiful, strong yet strange woman. Weakness seems to come so easily preying on my fears and loneliness. The strength that I fight for is a fight to stay strong, to move, to be alive and to embrace this stranger in my life.

Weakness has never been something I am comfortable with but this morning I seem to be chained in these memories and this weakness and these tears. Change and transformation release the chains. I am so afraid to listen to the words I am thinking and so afraid to feel the tears that are falling.

I will not be afraid of the memories of who I was or of this stranger and this strange life with which I have become intimate. This stranger has compelled me to leave it all behind and be bold in my newness. This stranger looks back at me in the mirror, imitating my face and body. She has crept into my heart and mind, shaping and molding them into her new home...into her new rhythm of single life. Suddenly this stranger has become my best friend. She has become...me.

Maybe this morning I will sit in my brown chair and feel the weakness leave with each tear and the strength come in with each word said in prayer. Sometimes it is good to sit in our weakness, in our loneliness so we can find strength from the one above. Sometimes we have to say goodbye to those memories that haunt us and threaten us in our change to become better. Sometimes we have to let go of what we know or who we are so we can discover what we need to know and who we can become. When we allow the stranger of transformation, it will know how to navigate the strangeness of life and the changes.

It does not matter how much I may want to go back—I can't. I cannot grow myself into what used to be. However, I can grow myself into what is now and what is going on at this moment. The brokenness is healed in the butterfly, not in the chrysalis. I cannot find freedom in the chrysalis or in the safe brown chair. I cannot find freedom in wanting things to be the same. I cannot find strength and hope unless I am willing to get out of the chrysalis. I cannot find strength and hope in staying the same when nothing around me is the same. I cannot find strength in what ifs. I release the chains by creating new memories and by releasing the what ifs. I become the beautiful butterfly by embracing a new way of living life. I get my wings to soar when I realize the pain I feel today will provide me with the strength to fly tomorrow and to break out of the chrysalis.

We cannot stay the same and move forward in life in a healthy and productive way unless we somehow come to the understanding that we are always changing and that everything and everybody around us is changing. We cannot live in the brown chair. We have to learn how to become different people with each change or we will die where we are. We will be thrown in the back of a truck, headed to the trash heap of other brown chairs, unless we change. Yes, change is scary but regret is scarier. Change is scary but not doing something about our lives when we can is scarier.

As my tears start to be spaced farther and farther apart and my tea is half gone, I think about how different I was a couple of years ago when sitting in my safe brown chair. It was Mark's favorite chair too. We would try to beat the other in gaining access to the brown comfy chair. It makes me smile, thinking of him in that chair. "My husband and I." It sounds like I am speaking a different language when I say those words. It has been difficult to let that part of who I was go being married and all. There is a lot different to this single life and walking in that door alone each and every night. Robert is gone…the dogs are gone…Mark is gone…my house is gone. Here I am by learning a different road and a different way of life I am learning how to love being alone. Besides, being alone with yourself is a good thing. It is like that quote by Ellen Burstyn, "What a lovely surprise to finally discover how unlonely being alone can be."

Another tear rolls down my cheek, this time splashing in my last sip of tea.

I do not know how to change. I am scared.

What do you mean you do not know how to change? You already have…and remember, it is your reality now, being single. It is a good reality for now. It is where your growth will occur.

It is so hard to look at…and to remember each detail of what you had, who you were and what you lost. You try hard to get the pieces back. You hope that if you can think about the way it was then maybe with a miracle you can stay there. You can sit in that brown chair and be that same person but reality always knocks the door in. It does not matter if it was locked or if you took the trouble to put a steel door around those comforting illusions…trying to keep the truth out. It will bust right through and confront you face-to-face, eye-to-eye, thought-to-thought, and tear-to-tear.

There are things that will forever change such as who we are. We have to embrace that change and learn how to become a different person by thinking differently. That is when we discover that we can choose to become the butterfly or to stay in the dark chrysalis. When a tragedy, challenge, barrier, or memories of the past threaten to make us weak and break us down, we have to change who we are and how we think.

We have to allow ourselves to do the hard stuff…you know…leave the shore…change the sails…change direction…swim against the current…take the path less traveled. Do what you don't want to do…but what you know will allow you to become stronger, better. Creating a new person…a new way of thinking…a new perspective…a new life…the butterfly.

Well…there they go, memories. Tea is all gone and tears are dried up. I do not think I can write another thought today. Wow, the time has passed so quickly sitting here thinking of what my life used to be like and who I once was. I am glad I made the choice to reel in those memories before they broke my line.

I think next time I want to avoid this brown chair. I think my new best friend will sit here that looks just like me yet is so much stronger, freer and more positive. I bet the tears will be tears of joy and the memories will be of what she accomplished that day. I bet she will not get caught up in the past and what she cannot change. If I had to guess, she will see this brown chair as a chance to write about how bright and different her today is and how much hope she has for the future. Let us continue what we are doing and keep moving on in this new life. Thank You, God, for always making me see the butterfly.

Images of Death and Life

"The fear of death follows from the fear of life. A man who lives fully is prepared to die at any time." —Mark Twain

It is hard to sleep with death images in your head, followed by a day of fractured thoughts. At times life and death seem separated only by a thin glass of sorts, which can be shattered at any time by a hard stone thrown.

Some friends and I went to spend time with a friend of ours who is dying of cancer. One of my friends said to me on the way home, "Dying is so ugly." I had to agree. The images of those headed to another life, images of Mark on the floor dying, the one I love leaving me, the fruitless effort of my breath exhaling into his lifeless lungs then nothing else mattering. The Images of other people I have been in the presence of when they leave their bodies behind. It was just the other night a friend from the gym passed from cancer. There was no resemblance of the person I once knew as I saw her lying in the casket. She fought so hard through this and some would say she lost the fight. Did she lose the fight or has she won?

Cancer…I hate it. My own journey with breast cancer brings the reality of my brush with what could have been death to my thoughts this night.

My friend from the gym called me back in February or March to ask me about the stomach pain she was having. She wanted to know if I had ever experienced anything like it, since we are both such avid gym rats. We talked a while and she asked me to pray with her, and I did. She called me a couple of weeks later. They had found something. She wanted prayer. She was so fearful that it was cancer. I told her not to let her fears go there and that she did not know yet. Not to assume the worst. I prayed with her. After that, I prayed for her. Her fear was so strong and she did not want to have cancer, as none of us would. Her worst fear came true.

How do we face our fears? I think we have to face them head-on so they do not rob us of living.

In April, it was official: She had cancer. Eight months later she lay dying. I did not keep up with her like I had intended over the months. Good intentions are nothing but that intentions of doing something. When we fail to follow through there are no longer intentions.

I saw her after her surgery, spoke with her a few times on the phone and prayed with her. My prayers seemed so empty to me. It is hard to understand sometimes is it not? It is hard to understand death, life, cancer and prayer.

I used to be quite the prayer warrior or so I was told. People always wanted me to pray for them. My prayer life is different now. My prayers go something like this now: Lord, have mercy on me. Thank You Jesus for this day. Jesus, forgive me for those I may have hurt as I forgive those who have hurt me. Help me love like You love me. Jesus, my friend needs You and I do not know what they need but you do so please do it for them. Protect my family and friends from the evil one. Protect me. You are my Shepherd and I shall not want. Jesus, please give me strength because I am done. Help me encourage someone today. Help me bring light to someone and help me be light. Jesus, my mom and dad need a hand. Jesus, my son is yours and I give him to you to love and take care of. Jesus, I cannot change the world but help me change myself and change my heart. I know you love us. I know you have won. Jesus, I just cannot see today through the death so I am glad you can. Tell Mark hello for me. God, bring peace to this world, bring love and may it start with me today.

My faith has turned into just being with Jesus and not a lot of doing with Jesus. All I know now is to be with Him in my day and allow Him to be with me. There is really nothing I understand anymore except that.

Sometimes there seems to be no rhyme or reason to any of it. But there is hope. You see, my friend is going home. She faced her greatest fear with courage, strength, fight, hope, love and dignity. She fought and she lived. The cancer thinks it has won. Death thinks it has won. But guess what? She won, Mark won and she is going home. She is going to her true home where there is no more death, pain, worries or fear.

She faced her fear with a strength that came from beyond. That body is not who she really is. The cancer that thought it had won in her body will be gone and she will be alive and well. We think about the ugliness of those we care about dying but there is really beauty. Beauty that they are taking off that body, leaving the ugliness behind and going on to something more beautiful than we who are left behind can even comprehend.

There is beauty in death if you look for it and if you understand that death is really the beginning of life. Seeing death while we are still here makes us appreciate life and a desire to live or at least it makes me feel this way. One has to live life to the fullest and give life everything you have. Do not stop the race before you reach the finish line, my friend finished her race strong.

Life can be fearful when you face it. However, there is still beauty in this world among all the thorns. As long as you are living you have a choice as to how you view this world. You have a choice as to how you are going to live the life you have to the fullest. I do not know about a lot of things but I do know that each minute we live our lives, we are faced with choices—all kinds of choices. Every choice we make has an impact on the kind of story we write, the kind of story we leave behind and the life we live. Our choices along with every thought make us stronger or weaker, healthier or sicker, more loving or hateful, more peaceful or more stressed-out. Each choice we make, we choose to be givers or takers. Each choice we make either muddies our waters or makes them clearer. Our thoughts and every decision has a domino effect in our lives. We are here for a purpose and even though we may not understand everything. Do we really need to understand everything? We only need to focus on our own choices, thoughts and beliefs.

This morning when I woke up, I said, "Linda, get up. Get going. You have so much to be thankful for." I read my index cards. One said: The Lord is my Shepherd; I shall not want. Another one said: You are going to feel like quitting—don't! One said: Winners never quit and quitters never win. The last index said: You are here for a purpose. Now go help someone.

I have come to realize it will be okay. God has a plan and it will all come together. Keep dreaming and remember that your home is where your heart is. Our real home is not here on earth, it is just a temporary place in which you are to shine, grow, love and share your gifts with others. Home is coming.

Today I went out the door with a smile to start my run. I was ready to conquer this year with my dreams and visions.

SWEET STRENGTH IS GETTING UP AND GOING NO MATTER WHAT.

Two Years

Well, Mark, it has been two years. Two long yet short years. Some days it feels like eternity since you've been gone, and some days it feels like you just left to go for that run and you will be back in forty minutes, like clockwork.

I am so happy that you made it home, bud…so happy. I do not know if you can see me down here. I know you are with me in some way because I have felt your presence especially when I am in the water. But I do not think you can see what goes on here because it would not be heaven if you could see all the suffering and pain on earth. Perhaps you just get a glimpse of the miracles.

Bud, it has been quite the obstacle course to maneuver on this path that has been set before me. The path that led away from being with you, married, safe, secure and protected from the stark path of today's reality. Single life again and making a living for myself. Some days I get so mad at you for leaving me. It is better now. As time goes on I am no longer mad at you. Who could stay mad at you anyway? I know the reality is that it was your time. God took you just as He will take all of us in a blink of the eye. Each breath is a gift.

We are here one day and then gone the next to another place that will be our real home. I often think about the impact you made on people's lives. You really loved those around you. Everyone misses you. You were my best friend. Even though we had our ups and downs, we were always there for each other. You were ALWAYS there for me through it all.

I just knew we were going to spend the rest of our long lives together especially since we went through so much together. Especially, during your first heart attack at forty-seven, when you said, "I know that God is going to relieve us of these financially draining condos now, because I had this heart attack." Well that did not happen. It just got harder after that. I am so sorry that you had to go through that. Our marriage sure got stronger over those last five years so I guess it was good to lose all of that stuff. We found out we did not need any of it anyway. Besides, I realized how little the loss of things, money and of homes. Where in comparison to losing someone I love. A person who was by my side every day.

Robert misses you so much. You would be so proud of him and what he has accomplished in the Navy. He looks after me as always and is worried about me. He has had a really difficult time and as mentioned in prior pages got a Mark the Shark tattoo on his back. Not sure how you would feel about the tattoo but I know you would be proud of him. You inspired him and loved him as your own. He could not have asked for a better Dad than you nor I, a husband. Today he texted me about how hard of a time he is having. He gets sick when he thinks of you and has an all too familiar punch in the stomach. The nausea feeling and knowing you are not here. What happened to our lives?

Change…it comes daily and we need to be ready to somehow embrace that change and have hope in the midst of the pain that there is a rhyme and a reason for everything and a purpose for all of this. That is what I believe.

Another Valentines Without You.

This is the third year without you on Valentines. The third year of being single on Valentines. Valentines Day was always very special for us. I still miss you but I am going to look at this Valentines differently.

I went for a run earlier today in the comfort of my sandy ocean asylum taking in the blue sky and the sunshine. I was making the time for reflection and contemplation of the love that was taken from me and the hope of the best future to come.

As I reached with my mind's eye into the depths of my heart and soul, I studied with intent the place that has been bound with loneliness and a distant lover who is no more.

I thought about the past years and how my heart has been laid bare. My heart, in the best way it could survive, tried and at times was unable to distinguish between loneliness, missing my best friend and attraction to someone new. Thinking of the times I wanted to believe the smooth talk slithering off the tongue of an unsung hero who seemed to be lonely too. I became wise as a serpent but longing to be gentle as a dove. I thought about the ups and downs, the highs and lows especially during this past year and the lessons learned, the emotions felt during this long trudge through the deep mud of loneliness.

As the run began, I pondered and thought about this Valentines. My heart began to beat a little faster, a smile came upon my face, and I realized the weight of dreading Valentines was gone. Some of the loneliness had gone out of my heart's door. There was a new word that became alive and in motion with each heartbeat: hope. Hope knows that the best is yet to be discovered. I became very aware of the strength that grew out of the loneliness and the lessons learned through determination. My smile increased, my run became lighter and a sense of confidence rose up in my soul. I am not really alone.

This Valentines, I am going to enjoy being with me and who I have become: a single, strong, independent woman soaring with the Son of God and enjoying every minute of where I am in life. I love every aspect of my life: my family, my friends and my work. It all reminds me that this Valentine's I am not really alone. It is only if I choose to be alone. Besides, I am so in love with the man who walks on water.

Rhyme or Reason

"This moment contains all moments" —C.S. Lewis

You know sometimes there is no rhyme or reason seemingly to life. Perhaps there is no rhyme or reason to death but there is always a reason to life. If we really live then we should not fear death. We have a purpose, a destiny, dreams to accomplish, passions to burn through, to love and embrace others, to walk and run the race marked out and to never give up. Life is a mystery and a miracle. Where time passes and our footprints are left behind.

It has been over two years since Mark died. Two years has also passed since Mark's friend, Hammond, died. Both were avid surfers to the same surfing fellowship, both great husbands, dads and both best friends to their wives. To us, it seems they left this earth a little too soon but there is a time for everything. Here on earth there is no rhyme or reason regarding time. However, God's time always is the perfect time. We trust the one who gives and takes time.

My son is home whom I love deeply as did Mark as his own. We were celebrating Mark's life together tonight and wanted others to celebrate their lives. Mark loved celebrating life. We solely spent a night of remembering two men and the very special footprints they left on this earth and in people's hearts. I did not know Hammond but Mark the Shark did. And I knew Mark and what a footprint he left.

What footprints do you want to leave behind? How do you want to be remembered? What would you do if you knew tonight would be your last?

Life is just a blink in the eye of our Creator but in our eyes it feels like a long journey. In reality it is a very short journey compared to everlasting life. Treasure every minute you are given to live and love others. Look around and breathe in every moment that you are graced with in this beautiful, astounding miracle of life that has been laid before you. Cherish the abundant life you have been offered to embrace by choice.

I have found such peace in who I am and who God created me to be and in being single once again. Treasuring the sweet memories and treasuring who I have become through life's treasured time.

SWEET STRENGTH IS LIVING, LOVING AND MOSTLY IT IS PEACE WITH WHERE YOU ARE TODAY!

The Monkey Lamp

"Neither is new wine put into old wineskins. If it is, the skins burst and the wine is spilled and the skins are destroyed. But new wine is put into fresh wineskins, and so both are preserved." —Jesus

In wellness coaching and life coaching we are always focused on moving the client forward. We are always focused on seeing what is already working in their lives and moving forward from that point. We never go back and try to fix something. Can you ever put things back to their original form? Can you ever make things the way they were? When something is broken we can never really fix it. We can try to put the pieces back together but they never really fit.

I remember one time when Mark was out of town after we had just married and moved in together. I decided to paint the whole house a different color. I would have never been brave enough to do this while he was home. Mark was not a man who liked change but I loved change. We would constantly go back and forth. I would move a piece of furniture around and when I got home it would be back in his favorite place. We eventually learned to compromise.

Mark had this favorite monkey lamp which was very sentimental to him. It was a beautiful lamp that I too loved. At one time we went through this monkey fetish. We would purchase just about anything with monkeys on it. Well, I thought the monkey lamp would give great lighting to my painting strokes in a room that was not well lit.

I was painting away and engrossed in the thought of how surprised and proud of me he would be when he walked in the door. His favorite lamp was resting on a small table with the cord stretched to the socket. Suddenly, our beloved miniature schnauzer decided to challenge the height of the cord and excitedly jumped over it to avoid walking through the maze of furniture so he could get to his favorite bed.

It was like a movie showing a scene in slow-motion. He tripped and the lamp slowly, slowly fell two feet that seemed like it took an hour in my dumbfounded haze. I reacted too slowly to swoop it up before it hit the hard tile floor where it shattered into pieces of sentiment and beauty. The monkey limbs and faces were now all over the floor. I stood stunned. My dog ran down the hallway, not looking back, in fear of the noise he had unknowingly caused.

I could hardly believe my eyes. Newly married, only wanting to please and surprise my husband with my hard work in our home. Now, the surprise was not the newly painted home but off the lamp lying in pieces across the floor. My heart sunk. My thoughts went straight to the familiar sounds after a mess up: How can I fix this? How can I make this better? What am I going to do? How do I tell him?

I decided I would call my friend as she surely would have the answer. Luckily my good friend had the answer...so now I have a partner in crime on my side. She suggested gluing the lamp back together and hanging a tassel around the top of the lamp. She was in interior design and she said it would work.

I got glue and started gluing piece by piece. I tried putting the lamp back together. Patience was my friend for the day. Once I finished, I put the lamp back in its familiar place on the nightstand by the bed and waited for Mark not to notice. I waited for the pieces to look glued and for my conscience to feel better. I waited and tried hard to not see the broken pieces. The first thing Mark noticed when he got into bed was the "fixed lamp." We survived the fixed lamp but we had to replace it with a new one and throw the old one out because it just never looked the same. It could not be fixed but it could be replaced.

The lamp was able to be replaced but humans are not replaceable. Although we cannot be replaced, we can move from the broken to a new creation. We cannot fix what has been broken. Nor can we go back and make anything what it was before. We cannot go backward but we can go forward by creating a new us, a new way of thinking and a new way of believing. Part of being broken is being able to acknowledge and realize that maybe it is not about fixing but instead about replacing it with and becoming something new.

Jesus talked a lot about new creation. He never said to go back and fix something. He said He was making all things new. If we focus on the broken then we focus on continually trying to fix something that is broken. How can we see the new that is before us? The broken gives us a new starting point, a new way of looking at things, a new way to see that it is not how we want to do it again. The broken is not about fixing but merely about starting over.

You Can't Do This

"Don't ask yourself what the world needs; ask yourself what makes you come alive. And then go and do that, because what the world needs is people who are alive." —Howard Thurman

"Every morning is a new beginning, a new chance for you to rewrite the story of your life." —Tina Su

I love my runs on the beach, and this morning was no exception. There is nothing like the feeling I get from being on the beach and having time to renew and refresh my thoughts. I love the fact that it is just me against myself. I love that no one makes me get out and run. There is no one there to make me run farther, faster or slower. It is just me, my mind, my thoughts, my body and my choice to continue or stop. I always feel empowered when I run that extra time or I stop and do some pushups when I really do not feel like it. Maybe should I switch to the soft sand for the last few minutes because I want to challenge myself. When I go that extra distance, in whatever form, I feel empowered to take the next step and I know I can. It is always a battle in your mind and in your thought process. It is just you and your thoughts. You can win the battle.

I love to encourage people, believe in people, and empower people to make the changes they want to make in their lives. Our thought process and what we believe about ourselves is so powerful that it can enable us to become the people we never knew we could become. It allows us to live out the dreams we thought were impossible or it can literally make us unable to move, unable to make a change or decision.

"People don't resist change. They resist being changed." —Peter Senge

Sometimes we just need someone to believe in us and encourage us, someone to be accountable to, someone to empower us and give us the confidence to make our own decisions.

There have been so many times during this journey I am on that I have wanted to quit. When the pain from losing Mark was so deep I felt like I could not move. Thoughts invaded my space, whispering to me, "You cannot do this by yourself. Who do you think you are? You cannot live without Mark." But I do not quit. I move and I go forward into life and truly live. I change my thought process to: You can do this, you are doing this and you will do this. Each time I choose to move forward in life it gets easier the next time. It gets easier to believe that I can. I have become empowered because I made the decision—no one else made it for me.

Change comes with each day. You have the power in each second to change. With each choice comes change, whether that choice is as simple as replacing soda with water, or replacing a sugary dessert with a piece of fruit. Maybe it is deciding to get up and walk for ten minutes instead of watching TV. Maybe it's deciding to get out of the bed. To put down that extra drink or to do that extra push-up. Each time you make the decision to push yourself you empower yourself to do it the next time and the time after that until you have won the battle. No one can do it for you. Do you really want them to?

Don't You Know?

The day before my husband's funeral a friend took me to get flowers to place in the vase that was going to be by my husband's ashes. As we were in the store, I passed people and people passed me. I of course was in a haze or whatever you want to call it. As thoughts echoed in my head, I wanted to scream, "Do you people realize I just lost my husband? Do you people realize the pain I am in? Can you hear the screaming in my heart? Can you see the shattered pieces dangling here on my sleeve? No, everyone was just going about their business buying groceries for their loved ones and probably going to cook dinner for their husbands. I wanted to scream, "I hate you! I hate the fact you still have your husband here."

You just never know what someone may be going through. That person who seems angry behind the cash register may have lost her husband, or wife, or child. The person who does not speak to you when you speak to them may be in a mental fog because of something horrific going on in their lives. Look beyond the emotions to the person's needs. Think about all the widows, orphans, those without shelter, those who have no one or no friends. Be a friend. Love others. Heck, go as far as to love your enemy. Pray for them. Pray for those who are hurting.

The past can really hold us back if we let it. It seems the past can become our future if we do not make it just that—the past. Even what you did a second ago is past. You cannot get it back and you cannot change it but you can change what you do with it and how you think or do not think about it. People get stuck in the past. There are those that cannot get past the anger, guilt, failure or mistakes. This will kill any hope of changing your life and making your future great. Every time you think of something unfavorable from the past you bring with it all the associated feelings and you cannot move forward. It will make you relive it again and again.

Do not let the past become your future. Even if it was a good past it is still the past. You cannot recreate it and the future holds more than you can even imagine if you will only press forward.

Can You Feel The Rain

"Some people feel the rain. Others just get wet." —*Bob Marley*

Last Friday I was out in the water attempting to surf and it was pouring rain. The waves were like rolling hills that had a beauty unbounded except by the limits of the shore. The waves had the appearance of gentleness but they were strong enough to achieve the surfer's desire to ride them.

I have begun in a very limited way to understand the connection of a surfer's soul to the music of the wave, the communication with nature and the bond with others in the water. I am not what I would call a true surfer yet. I am more of a beginner trying to figure it all out. However, what I have figured out is it helps me to feel the rain. It is a place I can find healing. It is a place I can find joy. It is a place that makes me listen and it silences my voice. It silences the world and silences everything when the wind is blowing and the waves are rolling in. I am in nature, in the rain and have a connection to the water. I have peace and a connection to God.

It was a piece of paradise in the water. It was a place of healing, of loving and feeling every pelting drop of rain in that downpour from heaven. I paddled out beyond everyone and laid on my board, stretched out and relaxed. A surrender. I surrendered to the business of life, the pressures of the journey, the precious pain of living and let the rain wash over me and cleanse me. The depths of all the ocean and what it holds was beneath me. I cried. I wept for the place offered to heal…to be with my thoughts…to be intimate with Jesus and His creation. I felt the rain…I was not just wet.

The Grief Encounter

"Grief is like the ocean; it comes in waves ebbing and flowing sometimes the water is calm, and sometimes it's overwhelming. All we can do is learn how to swim." —Vicki Harrison

I just got back from a run. I needed it to release another unexpected grief encounter. Sometimes I feel like I could run and never stop, run until my heart bursts and my legs collapse beneath me. Some days are just like that. No matter how strong your faith or how many friends surround you, you are on a journey to healing. There will be good days and not-so-good days but somehow the release comes from physically stretching your body to its limits heals pain. Healing is such a juxtaposition of physical strength and emotional fragility. It is a desire to be strong with a shattered and crushed heart. There is something about pain that helps us heal.

The good news is, tomorrow is a brand-new day with new hope, new strength and a new sunrise. I am so thankful for the pain that heals. I just heard Jesus whisper in my ear…He knows pain.

Home is Where the Heart Is

"Simplicity is making the journey of life with just baggage enough."
—*Charles Dudley Warner*

This weekend I went to my new home so I could measure the small humble abode (the model like mine) in which I will plant my new life and so I could once again contemplate what I need to purge from my material possessions.

This will be my third move in the last three and a half years. When Mark and I lost our 3,400-square-foot home and downsized to a 1,300-square-foot condo we purged and sold or gave away many material possessions. It was actually freeing after it was done.

After Mark died the owner sold the condo we were renting and I moved to a nine-hundred-square-foot space and purged once again. Now I am moving to a 670 square feet studio of pure paradise. I love the location of my studio and it will be brand new. It will be finished September 16, 2014 for my move date on September 27, 2014. It is brand new just like my new beginning.

I am looking forward to purging again and getting rid of material possessions. I have found that less is more. After losing three family members in one year it changed my thought process. Not a single one of my family members took any possessions with them. Naked they came into this world and naked they left it.

I am becoming keenly aware of the power of loving someone over loving a material possession.

We spend our lives collecting things only to realize that it is our hearts, our messages to others, our love for others and our interactions with others that are the real possessions we need to embrace. Because our loved ones are forever in our hearts. They leave memories that cannot be erased, stolen, rusted, or sold.

Does anyone really remember all the material things they have in their possession or recall everything they own or have owned? It would be hard to remember every piece of furniture, every dish and every piece of jewelry. I do not think anyone could unless they had pictures of the items or a list to refer to. However, I bet everyone can recall the people in their lives, ones they love, the memories these loved ones left with them and the impact these people have or have had in their lives because they are real. Relationships are real. Loved ones go on forever. The heart goes on forever. Material possessions have an ending and those possessions fade away.

It is difficult to decide what to take and what to give away because Mark and I shared most of what I have. Mark is not in those things. He is in
my heart.

For me, less is more. For me, following my heart is greater. For me, living this life to the fullest and giving my heart to others is sweeter than any possession I may have to purge.

No matter how little we feel we may be doing without, here in America there are those who have so much less. There are always people who have more. Be thankful for what you have both great or small and find peace in it and with it.

You have nothing to lose in possessions but your heart has everything to gain. Grow in heart and soul and follow your dreams.

Please Sit With Me

"Pain Hurts, sometimes important things come from sitting with your own pain." —Lynne Naraka

I can remember the initial pain, shock, and disbelief after Mark died. It was not what people said that eased that pain. It was the friends that just sat with me, cried with me, let me cry on their shoulders, hugged me, smiled at me and laughed with me it was simply their presence. Because there was nothing anyone could say that would take away the pain. Nothing. They would try to say things but it all seemed so useless. Some words seem to make it worse. There are several experiences people go through during which they really do not need a message full of words—they need a presence. Sometimes you just need to sit with people in their pain and love them and not try to fix them. Love them just where they are with a hug, a smile, a laugh or maybe you need to cry with them.

My Mom

My mom, I have only made a couple of entries about my mom. My wound is still fresh. It is hard for me to even grieve right now. I have felt the waves some, mostly small...but I am still really healing from my husband. I am really not even sure if I have grieved fully for my dad and my sister-in-law. It all happened too close together. I know that we expect our parents to go before us. However, I was not ready. Are we ever ready? My mom was one of the strongest women I have ever had the honor of meeting. She loved me and believed in me I could fill a book on everything the two of us have been through. There is nothing like a mother and daughter connection. I wish I could have talked to her. I never saw her conscious after her heart attack. I sang to her and read scripture to her while she lay unconscious. I believe with all my heart she heard me. God just works like that. Furthermore, I know that the grief will come and time will release it as it needs to be released. I will be ready to embrace the waves when they come and let the tears flow as needed. However, I have learned staying in that state is not where I want to live nor would those who loved us and went before us. Life is for the living. As I have said many times before, if we have a heart beat we have a purpose and let us live it out (I wrote this in January 2016).

Mom Waiting To Go Home.

"My mother taught me about the power of inspiration and courage, and she did it with a strength and passion I wish could be bottled."
—Carly Fiorina

As I took a break in the earthly sensory garden at Hospice Hospital. I sat contemplating life and death.

My Mom is still waiting to go home. So she can be at peace.

There are so many things in this life that are out of our control and many things we try to control. We are always trying to get on the path that makes it happen. Whatever that path is for us. We want to make our own path to the pain, the lessons, the failures, the guilt and the loss. Consequently, if only we would stay on the path that was chosen for us then we would find peace, our destiny and our wholeness at the end of the path.

May we journey on the path laid out before us. The sensory path of grace, faith, hope and peace.

God I Miss Her.

Well now it is a different morning but a new day. One of reflection, of another change, of another challenge to move forward in strength and love despite loss. The prayers, texts and calls I received made a difference in my journey with Mom. Sweet Strength is what I received from them.

On May 13, 2015, my mom died at the age eighty-three years old. My oldest brother had taken Mom to the hospital early in the morning. She was having chest pain. They admitted her, ran some tests but did not see immediate concern in the first test. However, the second test's results indicated she was having a heart attack. They ran to her room only to find her unconscious. They shocked her heart and got her breathing but it was too late Mom had suffered brain damage. She had been put in a room with no heart monitor, an eighty-three-year-old woman with a pacemaker complaining of chest pain.

She was transferred to another hospital better equipped to handle heart conditions. By the time I got there it was early morning. My brother had called me at around two in the morning, telling me to meet him at the new hospital. I drove the two-hour route and made it. There she was, hooked up to a respirator. She was not breathing on her own, even though her heart was still strong. It was so sad. I knew that was not what she wanted. She had made that clear.

The doctors wanted to try a procedure that could possibly reverse the brain damage. They would take her body back down to freezing and warm her up; the whole process took twenty-four hours. There were risks, of course, but at that point it was worth taking those risks. I remember laying on her saying, please do not go yet, do not die. Then feeling guilty for those words. I knew that was unfair. Unfair to ask her to stay beyond what she could. She needed to hear the word it was okay. It was okay to let go. In my selfishness I was putting a barrier on her release to be with dad. The procedure did not work and on Mother's Day we removed her from the respirator. She had no hope of recovery. It was a difficult decision no one would want to make on Mother's Day or any other day. We later found out the heart attack would not have killed her; the culprit would have been the lack of oxygen going to her brain. The reality is it was her time, she was preparing to go home. God in his mercy was getting her ready for paradise.

We called in hospice and I stayed with Mom until her death a week and a half later. She never regained consciousness. I sang to her, read scripture to her—I think I only left her side for one night.

I was a little more prepared for the funeral home this time because I had been there so many times. I guess prepared was the word I substituted familiar with. Three years had passed now allowing me to adjust to loss. Somehow, I felt like I could actually help with my mother's arrangements. The unfamiliar was becoming familiar. The arrangements and the changes were becoming a new normal.

It was a beautiful celebration of life for my mom yesterday. I was both honored and privileged to be a pallbearer alongside my two brothers, son and two cousins. We carried her body to its final resting place. She and Dad are together again, along with my husband, my sister-in-law and all the other family and friends who have gone to paradise, a place full of unconditional love, amazing grace and incredible, indescribable joy and beauty.

There is an indescribable connection between a mother and her daughter that is like no other. I cannot bear the thought of being without my mom during the next half of my journey but it was her time. She was finally reunited with Dad.

My mom was so strong and very smart. I miss her so much. We had some great times together. We talked pretty much every day. She was my best friend growing up. We did so many things together and we used to even exchange clothes. She was a very snappy dresser and she and I wore the same size. She was always smiling. I really want to write a story about her life one day and all the good times. I am happy she is whole and has been healed with pure love, joy and eternal life.

My son was such a great help to me during this time. He was there for me and let me break down on several occasions while he held and comforted me. He was once the boy I held in my arms and now he was holding me in his.

One day last week when I was at my lowest point, I was talking to a friend. He said that the one who created us breathes life into us, delivers us from evil, loves us unconditionally, gives us gifts, purpose and meaning by His grace. It is through his mercy He carries us home to be with those we love and will forever and ever.

How could that not give me peace? I will miss my mom so much but that pain needs to be recycled into something positive and good because she is home now and happier than she has ever been.

Death and separation are only for a short time. Our family reunion at the banquet feast of pure love is and will be eternal.

I will see you again Mama, Daddy, Mark and Donna when I get home. I love and miss you. R.I.P.

Jeep

I have needed extra beach therapy this month and made it a point to squeeze it in. Meeting God there is just so healing.

I am so sad, my 1999 Jeep Cherokee is headed to the junkyard. I was so attached to that Jeep. I knew better than to get attached to a material possession. After all, it is just that—a material thing. It is an illusion that we own them. They can be taken away at any time. We cannot take any of it with us when we depart from this world. There is a story behind my Jeep and that story is enmeshed in my heart and memories. My husband and I bought it when we sold our previous car before it got repossessed when we were losing everything. We did not have enough cash to buy the 1999 Jeep Cherokee. We were short $1,500.00 so the previous owner took the amount needed, $1,500, from an emerald ring my husband had bought for me. The Jeep was that emerald ring that Mark had bought for me in St. Thomas. He had surprised me with it on our vacation there. It was a birthday gift!

It is my fault. I wrecked it Memorial Day weekend. Just found out today that it will cost too much to fix it. I tried everything to keep it but the insurance company declared it as being totaled. I was told this in unemotional language. People that are detached from it and know its material value…not its heart value. The good news is that no one was hurt, thank goodness. Now I have to find another vehicle. It is not the best time to get another car but God is always on time. So I have to trust. I have no idea what to get because I loved that Jeep. But I really do need a new car and this will be a great new beginning. I always look for those beginnings because that is what life is really about—beginnings.

So I am giving up my Jeep as it is time for another journey and onto my next adventure! I am thankful that I have been given precious memories that hold my hand and heart during beach therapy. Hard times are just a test and I like passing the test.

This, too, shall pass and life continues. You have to learn how to continue with more strength, more thankfulness and a greater love of life.

Chock full o' Nuts

"He who has a why to live for can bear almost any how."
—*Friedrich Nietzsche*

It is the little things that make you smile. Those who have lost loved ones can relate to this.

Robert is still sleeping. He is on night shift. I have not drank coffee in over four years. However, this morning I decided I would sit and have a cup of coffee since I have no beach to walk on. I opened the cabinet and bam, Mark's coffee that he would drink every morning!

Robert is drinking the same thing which made me smile and made a tear fall. I would try to get Mark to try other types of coffee but he loved his Chock full o'Nuts. How about the tag line? "The heavenly original coffee."

I wonder if Mark is having his coffee which he loved to drink in the mornings before going to check the surf. He was not ever in a hurry, something we could all learn from.

I can just picture him sitting at that big, long banquet table with his mom and dad, my mom and dad, his aunt and uncle, Donna, some of our friends, our dogs (Sugar Ray, Becker and Evander, looking for treats that fall from the table), Andy Irons among other surfers and Jesus telling stories. They are all laughing and so full of love waiting to greet and then all of us when we get home. Mark is asking Jesus to come surf with him. Can you picture it? The crystal-clear colors, smells and sounds. The indescribable unconditional love that we strive for here is there in perfection. They have reached it. We think we loved them here but can you imagine the peace they feel with the laughter and smiles radiating in each healed soul? The peace that transcends all understanding that they have. Every single heart's desire is there in the stories, and in the laughter at the banquet table of the unique spirits and souls. All together as one.

They are cheering us on. They are pulling for us and whispering to us, "You got this! Your journey is short, enjoy it." They want us to love and be loved here. They want us to experience joy, laughter and purpose. They want us to live here, now.

In heaven there is beauty, love, laughter, no more pain or suffering and no more tears where they are forever in paradise.

We do not need to wait until heaven to experience love, peace and paradise. We can create it here by changing one person: ourselves. Let us all take time to sit, read and be thankful for a cup of Chock full o'Nuts.

Flowers That Live Forever

"Here was a flower strangely like itself and yet utterly unlike itself too. Such a paradox has often been the basis for the most impassioned love."
—*Thomas M. Disch*

I have to be vulnerable and admit that the holidays are just not my favorite. This is my third year without my husband and it really is not the same. That does not mean I sit around and feel sorry for myself— far from it. I stay very engaged with life. Besides, if you look around there are many people in far more difficult circumstances.

Some flowers of the heart live on and bloom year after year— artificial flowers which are unaffected by time, planted in the soil of memories and harvested when needed to feed the hunger of missed love.

One Sunday, my husband picked a bouquet of flowers off of the sidewalk in a parking lot and handed them to me through my car window. He said, "I picked these just for you. I love you." We had a chuckle together. I said, "Oh…I just love them." He died of a heart attack the next day. I brought the flowers out for the holidays, as a reminder of the grace and love of both God and Mark. You see, God knew Mark would be gone from me the next day. He knew I loved it when Mark brought me flowers and he knew that these last flowers I would receive would never die just like Mark—away from me but very much alive.

God is good all the time and all the time He is good.

SWEET STRENGTH. MAKE IT SWEET AND KEEP IT STRONG.

"Like A Stone, Time Rolls On." (Eric Church)

I wrote these words on Facebook on December 31, 2011. As Mark stood behind me (waiting on me for once instead of me waiting on him) he said, "Linda you need to write a book." I said, Mark, what would I write about? He said to me, "Linda you have a lot to write about, I am telling you need to write a book." Honey, I did what you said, I have written a book for you. Here is what I wrote that night:

"Headed out to dinner with my favorite surfer guy! I am so blessed! I hope your New Year Challenges you to look beyond your mud puddles…into a vast and wide open sea of beauty and change."

Wow, words are powerful! Little did I know that in nine days Mark would be dead. He was dead in flesh but alive in spirit. Total perfection after running the race of life or surfing the waves of life. I would be living the very words I wrote trying to look beyond my mud puddles that lie ahead over the next years.

Time is a phenomenon that escapes every grasp at trying to contain it, stop it, forget, move it, rush it, slow it down or speed it up. Time is like a stone it rolls on.

Mark was never on time. When he died he had 5 watches on his nightstand. They certainly did not give him an edge on being on time when his friends called him to surf or being on time when we went places. They were a style for Mark. A style that only Mark had. The only time Mark showed up on the very second he was to be somewhere was when God called him home. He was not late. It was his time. He went from the clock time here. The twenty-four hours that go tick tock to eternal time where he is always on time now.

Mark was loved. In fact, Mark made everyone feel like they were his best friends. I have to tell you something, I miss Mark's friendship more than anything. I miss his encouragement and his belief in me when I did not believe in myself. We were far from perfect in our marriage and just like any couple or any relationship we had our challenges no matter how in love you are with someone marriage takes work from both partners. The one thing Mark and I did together was that we never gave up on each other. We were best friends. He was such an incredible friend. He loved slowing down and talking to people. If he saw you, he would talk to you as if you were his best friend. You were his focus. That is a gift. Everyone loved Mark. I miss him so much.

He loved going down to the beach to the surfing spot where 64th and 65th avenue joined and just hung out with his surfing buddies. Nothing gave him more joy. He used to tell a story about when he was in high school dating a girl and she wanted him to go to her house and watch T.V. with him. He said that on that particular day the waves were pumping so Mark told her he was going surfing instead. She said, "It's me or surfing." He said he drove her home. He then got out of the car and went around to her side when he opened her door and said, "Goodbye." LOL. I can relate to her. I was told goodbye many days to surf. LOL.

We always think we have all this time with our loved ones. We always think they will be there the next day and the next day. Time is like a stone it rolls on and if you are not careful that stone will pull you under.

Mark loved the water, others in the water with him and he had a community of surfers. He loved helping the gromes, which is a name referencing the younger surfers. They all loved him, "Mark the Shark." The only time Mark was fast was on the wave in the water. I am going out as I do every Jan. 9th and paddle out in memory of the man who showed me what it was to be a best friend. I know he is watching me and he would love me getting out there and surfing for him. Waves or no waves.

I often wonder what Mark would say about everything today. Little did he know when he named my business Sweet Strength, that I would need that sweet strength for the next four years to live my life with. I wonder if he would even know me or recognize me. I have changed so much. I am not the same woman I was four years ago. I became a new person on that day when I was thrown into another time. I have learned more about myself these last four years than I ever did in the fifty before. Mark taught me so much while he was alive. I had no clue how much I learned from him until he was no longer here. He would not know that or think that he had that impact. I did not know either until the imprints you left not only on me but Robert, my family and your community of friends will never be forgotten. Your legacy of integrity, character, honesty, loyalty, strength and kindness lives on in the hearts of those who were honored enough to know you.

Four years is much too long to see that smile and hear that laugh but we will all see you when we get home. Surf on and I hope that I have made you smile over the last four years. I hope you are watching me today when I am on the water!!!!

SWEET STRENGTH. MAKE IT SWEET AND KEEP IT STRONG. CARRY ON.

Whole Again

"Pay mind to your own life, your own health, and wholeness. A bleeding heart is not help to anyone if it bleeds to death." —Frederick Buechner

I went to Myrtle Beach last night because sometimes I just need to see Billy Perry. You see he is Mark's only living blood relative. The only one. When I see Billy it feels as if I have visited Mark in some way. They grew up together. I am so grateful for Billy's stories and his closeness to Mark. It has been over four years since Mark my husband died. The love you have for someone never dies. You have a longing to see them again and maybe catch a glimpse of them in the story of another about them. Billy, I love you. Thank you for always being there. At times the stories help to piece together what seems to be missing…and sometimes it makes you feel whole again.

You really do become whole again but in a different way. Because, you will never look at life or your life or others' lives in the same way. You are always hopeful it is a positive light that comes out of the grief. Because I could not get my sweet strength any other way except to find the hope and good in a tragedy.

I think it gives you a higher respect of life, hope, love and peace. You are just changed. For me it has been a new awakening into what is important. I have found that love is literally the most important thing. The love of another, empowering one another to live our dreams and to give to others.

Mark's love for me has helped me so much. I can love again. It will be a different kind of love and it is okay. My next relationship will look and will be different and that is okay. We are all going to be seated soon enough at the banquet table anyway.

Hearts enmeshed in amazing grace, undeserved mercy, unconditional love based on no conditions and perfect peace. When I am called home then I will be grounded. Home is where the heart is . . .

You cannot go back but you can take all the love, memories, pain, heartache and make it blossom into a beautiful new spring.

May you find solitude, peace and love in the ever changing journey you are on even in the loss and pain.

A New Normal

I know this transformation is painful, but you're not falling apart; you're just falling into something different, with a new capacity to be beautiful.
—*William Hannan*

You can decide to live in your loss or move into your new beginning, a new normal. It is a choice we all have. We can decide to recycle our pain. That is what I have chosen to do with the book I am writing and life coaching. I am using my pain to empower others and to achieve their dreams. I am determined to continue this journey by living out my dreams and helping others live theirs.

I have continued to move forward in the midst of grief. At fifty, I started over in every way. If I can do it anyone can. I started my business Sweet Strength. I learned to surf, moved to a new location to get a new start, joined Toastmasters (speaking club), trademarked Sweet Strength, completed a website, went out of the country twice by myself and wrote my first book. I have participated in four NPC Masters Figure Contests and placed in every one. It has been with the help of coaches, friends and family, who have inspired me to continue the journey that is before me. Without God, friends and family I could not have found the Sweet Strength that lies inside and helps me continue to press forward.

You always have more Sweet Strength in you than you know you just have to be willing to find it. It is not who you think you are that holds you back it is who you think you are not. Our words and thoughts create our reality but the good news is that just with a thought we can recreate our reality. Be aware of what you are thinking about and use that white towel not to surrender but to wipe the sweat off so you can go the extra round. Be better than you were yesterday, taking it day by day.

I often tell people you will not be able to love others until you learn to love yourself. You cannot take care of others until you take care of yourself. And you will never live out your dreams—who you want to be and what you want to do—until you learn to smile and take responsibility for your actions. Become the victor, not the victim.

Life is truly what you make it. Those who have gone before us would be the first to say: live it to the fullest and make each day count.

"You are always one choice away from changing your life."

The Memories:

Photos

In Loving Memory of my Husband and Best Friend, Mark "the Shark"
November 13, 1958 - January 9, 2012

About the Author

Linda Timmons currently resides in Mount Pleasant, SC with her husband Breeze Timmons. She also now owns Sweet Strength Fitness Studio where her husband works with her. Linda is an experienced and skilled trainer and life coach. She is always challenging herself to better serve her clients. Currently, Linda holds the following certifications:

- Certified Fitness Trainer, ISSA
- Certified Nutrition Coach, ISSA
- Certified Transformation Specialist, ISSA
- Certified Wellness/ Health Coach, Wellcoaches
- Certified Women's Fitness Specialist, NASM
- Certified Lifestyle Medicine Coach, American College of Lifestyle Medicine
- Professional Life Coach, PCCI

To Contact & Learn More About Linda:

Website: www.sweetstrength.com
Facebook: www.facebook.com/sweetstrengthcoaching
Email: linda.sweetstrength@gmail.com

Made in the USA
Columbia, SC
23 December 2023

28496953R00093